BURY
MURDERS

BURY
MURDERS

SEAN FRAIN

The
History
Press

First published 2014

The History Press
The Mill, Brimscombe Port
Stroud, Gloucestershire, GL5 2QG
www.thehistorypress.co.uk

British Library Cataloguing in Publication Data.
A catalogue record for this book is available from the British Library.

ISBN 978 0 7524 8871 4

Typesetting and origination by The History Press
Printed in Great Britain

CONTENTS

Introduction   6

Case One   1825   A Vicious Double Murder   8

Case Two   1866   A Shocking and Violent Murder   15

Case Three   1887   A Frenzied Attack   29

Case Four   1889   A Murder of Tremendous Violence   35

Case Five   1900   Murder?   44

Case Six   1900   A Callous Murder that Shocked the Nation 50

Case Seven   1900   The Bury Lamp Tragedy   62

Case Eight   1901   A Cruel and Atrocious Murder   66

Case Nine   1903   Death of a Sweetheart   73

Case Ten   1914   The Attempted Murder of a Neighbour   79

                        Four Cases of Murder and Suicide   85

INTRODUCTION

Bury is famous for a number of reasons, such as its 'world-famous' market, its strong links to industry, and its leading industrialists such as Sir Robert Peel, both father and son. More recently, Bury has produced a number of famous people too, including celebrities from the world of music, comedy, drama and football, such as the group Elbow, Victoria Wood, Steve Halliwell, who made the character Zak Dingle in *Emmerdale* all his own, and the Neville brothers, who have enjoyed distinguished football careers for both Manchester United and England. But Bury is also infamous in many ways, though such infamy has mostly been buried, no doubt in the hopes that it will just go away. Bury's infamous past, however, is as much a part of the history of the town as its triumphs, and should be recorded before it is forgotten forever. This is not in any way to glorify such events, but simply because true history should be recorded and, in the case of this book which focuses on murders in and around the town, because the names of the victims should not be wiped from the pages of history. They should be remembered and their terrible sufferings should be mourned.

When I first began researching the criminal history of Bury, I was astounded at not only the number of murders that have occurred, but at the sheer viciousness and callousness of some of these crimes, which are truly horrific and defy human logic and reason. You will understand my shock as you read through these terrible yet fascinating accounts, for surely the deepest imaginings of any sane person could not come up with such awful plots for other human beings, in many cases close relatives. Bury is thus infamous for such evil acts committed by a very select few of its residents and the crimes themselves, the court cases that followed and the sentences passed, feature in this book.

I was surprised to discover that a resident from the Bury area was the first person to be hanged in Manchester and I was even more surprised to discover the reaction of the public who made this hanging into a national event; some might even say a circus. Certainly, people's attitudes towards criminals back in those days was far different to today, when those who commit such horrific and evil acts are often back on our streets and among society after serving only a few short years in prison. What struck me about Victorian times in particular, was that criminals who committed serious crimes such as murder were dealt with severely and promptly. Their trial was sometimes within weeks, sentence was quickly passed if found guilty and a very short time later the hanging itself took place.

Please be aware that some of the buildings featured in this volume are private dwellings and as such the reader is advised not to trespass on the property.

Sean Frain, 2014

CASE ONE   1825

A VICIOUS DOUBLE MURDER

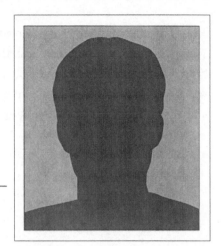

Suspect:	John Diggles
Age:	?
Charge:	Murder

Benjamin and Alice Cass were a happily married couple who lived at Birtle-cum-Bamford and by the year 1825 they were 64 and 80 years of age respectively. Benjamin Cass was a farmer, but by this time he was farming in a much smaller way than in previous years. His had been a prosperous establishment over the years and he had invested his profits wisely in property. He owned a number of cottages which he rented out and Saturday, 1 October 1825 was the due date for rents, though some of his tenants were in arrears.

Birtle-cum-Bamford was then a very rural idyll. The area today remains rural where farms and the occasional mill are located, though the urban sprawl from both Bury and Heywood has reached into what was once a mostly uninhabited region. The nearest neighbour to Benjamin and Alice Cass was at least a mile away and farming settlements were scattered about. Benjamin and Alice resided on the land they owned, but both were now getting rather frail and a neighbour of theirs would often sit with them on an evening and help out where possible.

On Saturday, 1 October 1825 a small number of people had brief contact with Benjamin Cass, and the lady who sometimes visited the ageing couple arrived later in the day and sat with them until 10 p.m. Benjamin was obviously a religious man, as when she was going she noticed that he had picked up his prayer book to have a read before retiring for the night. Alice was just beginning to undress, in preparation of putting on her night attire.

Birtle-cum-Bamford today.

She was just taking off her stockings when the visitor, unnamed in old newspaper articles recounting the events of that night, said goodnight and closed the door behind her as she went on her way home through the dark countryside.

Benjamin's brother, Joseph Cass, was up and about early on that Sunday morning. He lived a couple of miles from his brother and went to see him first thing, arriving at the farm a little after 6 a.m. just as it was coming light. Being farmers they were obviously accustomed to being up and about early each day. Unusually, there was no sign of anyone astir and so Joseph opened the unlocked door and went inside. The interior was still quite dark, but he could just make out the form of his brother and his wife sat on chairs, but apparently asleep. Alice had her head on her husband's shoulder and both did not move as Joseph Cass entered the room.

Joseph tried to rouse the couple, using his voice at first, and then went over to shake them awake. It was then that he realised the pair were dead and that they had severe wounds about their heads. Blood was also on his hands. In a panic he ran from the house and went off to fetch a neighbour called John Chadwick. They arrived back about 15 minutes later and a truly horrific scene greeted them now that it was almost fully light and they could see the interior of the room.

The head of Benjamin was 'almost clove in two'. His nose was almost completely severed from his face, hanging by a thread of skin, his chin severely cut open. The skull of Alice, who was seated next to her husband with her arms round his neck, was laid open and parts of her brain were scattered about the floor, her face badly bruised. A blood-spattered spade and poker lay on the floor nearby. It was obvious that the killer, a particularly sick and twisted individual, had placed the bodies in that position after the gruesome and horrific attack had ended.

The authorities were called in and their immediate thoughts were that the motive was unlikely to have been robbery, as a watch lay on the table in the room where the attack had taken place which could not have been missed by someone intent on stealing from the old couple. It was soon discovered that some people owed rent to Benjamin and this was considered as a possible motive for the murders. Enquiries by the authorities were fruitless regarding those who owed rents to Benjamin, due on the very day of his murder, but leads directed the investigations to the City of Manchester some ten miles or so from Bury. However, it seems such leads ended in disappointment. Any kind of dodgy dealings on the part of Benjamin which could have led to a motive for his murder were

'a truly horrific scene greeted them'

also ruled out, as people who knew him well were all of the same opinion; Benjamin Cass was an honest and peaceable man who was highly unlikely to have made enemies of those he dealt with.

At Halifax a man named John Diggles visited a number of people he knew and tried to sell them a pair of shoes, a suit, waistcoat and a pair of spectacles. How the authorities heard of this is unspecified in accounts written at the time, but possibly one of the several folk who were approached by Diggles may have heard of the murders at Bury. Knowing Diggles had been in that area and seeing him attempting to sell clothes that obviously did not belong to him, they might have contacted the local authorities who then contacted the authorities in Bury. However it happened, John Diggles was arrested at Halifax and taken back to Bury where he was questioned about the murders.

Reports written immediately after the arrest, which tended to be sensationalised, stated that Diggles then confessed to the murder. However, such reports proved to be inaccurate, as we shall see. He actually confessed to being near to the scene of the crime, but pointed a finger at a chap called Ralph Weston, telling the authorities that it was him who had committed the terrible deed. According to Diggles, he had waited with Ralph Weston in a nearby meadow and on seeing the neighbour that had sat with the old couple that evening finally leave about 10 p.m., Weston headed off to the cottage, telling Diggles that he 'wanted something'. The court was later told of how Alice was still in a state of half-undress, as she was when the neighbour had left the old couple, when she was killed, showing the murderer was watching the cottage and awaiting his chance. John Diggles denied knowing anything about the murders.

Ralph Weston was thus arrested, but he was most vociferous in denying he had anything to do with the murders and that he could provide a solid alibi to prove it. This alibi appeared at the inquest a few days after the murders and Ralph Weston was acquitted. John Diggles now stood alone and was found guilty of the murders of Benjamin and Alice Cass at the inquest. The magistrates came to the same conclusion and Diggles was committed to trial at the notorious Lancaster Castle, where few killers escaped the hangman's noose. Diggles was then transferred to Lancaster Castle, awaiting his trial, the date of which was set for Thursday, 16 March 1826.

The trial was part of the Lancaster Spring Assizes and John Diggles pleaded not guilty before the court, with Mr Williams and Mr Tindal appearing for the Crown. Diggles continued to implicate Ralph Weston, but Weston had not just one solid alibi, but several, and continued to vociferously protest his innocence in the matter.

Several people gave evidence that day, including a Bury surgeon named Joseph Goodland. He had examined the bodies and found that the head injuries, those about the skull, had caused the deaths of both Benjamin

Above and below: Two views of the lane where this shocking double murder took place.

and Alice Cass. The skulls of both victims had been severely fractured and there were injuries to the upper part of the head of Alice. Bones were also fractured, but these were not fatal injuries. Several cuts and bruises were also found on the bodies, but these alone would not have proved fatal. Severe blows to the head with the spade and poker had been to blame for their deaths. This was important in establishing that a mere fight had not broken out after a row over rents, or some other matter. Murder was obviously the intent from the beginning, as this was in no way a matter of self-defence. The attack was vicious and sustained and could only have resulted in the deaths of the victims.

Those whom John Diggles had attempted to sell clothes to also appeared as witnesses, and the articles of clothing in question were on display in the courtroom, where they were formally identified by the witnesses and shown to the jury. Clear evidence was given that the shoes, suit, waistcoat and spectacles had all been in the possession of John Diggles and that he had tried to sell them at various locations around Halifax. One of the most damning witness statements was that made by William Cass, the uncle of Benjamin Cass. He identified the shoes and the jury was certain of his testimony, as he was a cobbler by trade and had actually made those shoes for his nephew. He could not have been mistaken.

A Bury tailor also testified in court, stating that he had made the suit for Benjamin Cass which was shown to the jury. Thomas Cromplin was his name and he was certain those were the clothes he had made for Benjamin Cass. Other witnesses also testified in court that they had seen John Diggles walking along various roads leading away from Bury carrying a large parcel. Coupled with the testimony of those witnesses in Halifax whom Diggles had approached in an attempt to sell various items belonging to Benjamin Cass, it was obvious that Diggles had carried them from Bury into West Yorkshire. The fact that he had clothing and other items, such as the spectacles, that belonged to one of the victims of the atrocious double murder was by this time undisputable.

John Diggles, after all other testimonies had been heard, was allowed to speak for himself. No matter what questions were put to him he continued to return to the subject of Ralph Weston, determined to continue pointing the accusing finger. He remained adamant that Weston had been the one who had gone to the Cass cottage while he had waited in the nearby meadow, but the judge was having none of it, completely dismissing Diggles' cries of innocence and informing the jury that Ralph Weston had solid alibis, which had resulted in his complete acquittal.

The jury was now asked to deliberate and they retired to do so. Having heard some pretty damning evidence they did not have to consider for too long and reached their decision after only 30 minutes. They were soon back in the courtroom, where the verdict was read. They found John Diggles guilty of willful murder and all that was left now was for the judge to pass sentence.

There was complete silence at the Lancaster Assizes as His Lordship placed the forbidding black cap on the top of his head and began to pass sentence. John Diggles had shown no remorse whatsoever and to the end had denied killing the unfortunate old couple, so he was shown no mercy by the judge. His Lordship passed the death sentence, stating that he should be hanged within 48 hours, but set the date for Monday, 20 March 1826, saying that the killer should have more time to ponder on what he had done. He also said that the body of John Diggles would be given over to surgeons for dissection. An attitude of good-riddance to bad rubbish prevailed at the culmination of this horrific and gruesome case.

Additional Notes:

Immediately after the arrest of John Diggles for the murder of Benjamin and Alice Cass, the sheer shocking nature of the crime seemed to spark a frenzy of media attention and those early reports needed to be taken with more than a pinch of salt. Diggles had supposedly implicated three other men in the crime, naming two, but refusing to provide the name of the other perpetrator. Also, reports consistently stated that Diggles had confessed to the murders, but at no time did he do so. He never confessed, as far as can be ascertained, even up to the point of death on that fateful Monday in March when he at last swung from the hangman's rope. His had been a vicious attack that had shocked and horrified the nation, not just local folk.

SOLVED

CASE TWO 1866

A SHOCKING AND VIOLENT MURDER

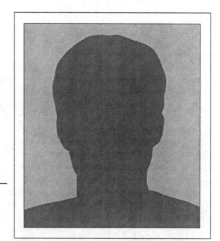

Suspect: James Burrows

Age: 18

Charge: Murder

John Brennan was an Irishman who had come to England to find work so he could provide for his wife and six children and keep them out of the workhouse, where conditions were often so bad that many chose to live in dire poverty on the streets rather than enter. Brennan was not a skilled man according to society's viewpoint, regarded as a humble farm labourer. However, he was a very skilled man in reality as he was a ploughman,

The Bury Workhouse, which is now part of Fairfield Hospital.

Two more views of what was the Bury Workhouse.

a position that required training and handling of horses, as well as carrying out the actual job of ploughing.

Furrows had to be cut straight and the equipment used had to be maintained and handled correctly. For instance, when more than one horse was used, which was frequently, the yoke had to be set just right, so that both horses put in the same amount of work. This would prevent one doing more than the other and becoming either exhausted, or even injured, which would have resulted in a much shorter working lifespan. Horses had to earn their keep on farms before the coming of the tractor and many, many years of work could be expected of any horse that was looked after well and that was worked wisely and considerately. Brennan was highly skilled, but in those days work was not secure because of changing farming fortunes (nothing has changed, it is the same today) and so John Brennan found himself out of work on English shores with six hungry children to feed and clothe, not to mention to keep sheltered.

A suitable job did become available at a farm in the Hopwood area of Bury, which was a district of Heywood, yet another borough of Bury in those days, and John Brennan applied for the position of farm labourer that also included ploughing work. He was successful in securing the position and his employer was a Mr Burrows who owned the farm, as well as a nearby public house called the Hopwood Arms. Burrows also owned a small brewery that supplied his public house with ale. He must have been an affluent man and no doubt Brennan believed he had secured for himself a secure position at the Burrows farmstead.

Mr Burrows gave John Brennan a starting date of Monday, 21 May 1866. Brennan was 40 years of age at the time and had plenty of previous experience of working on farms, so Mr Burrows put him to the plough, literally speaking, right away. That Monday, his first day of work at the Burrows farm, saw him putting a collar on a single horse and leading it out to the fields for ploughing. John Brennan must have been content at the time, knowing he was providing for his family and enjoying the excitement that comes with starting a new job, even if it was something he had been doing for many years previous to this. He got stuck into his work and the ploughing of the field moved ahead steadily, the furrows straight and true, as was befitting of an experienced ploughman who took pride in his work.

James Burrows was the 18-year-old son of the publican and gentleman farmer and he had grown into rather a disappointment to his father, as he could not read and write and spent most of his days drinking. He was a gambler and a drunkard and often slept out at night, either sleeping in stables or any convenient hayloft he could get into. While the hardworking and conscientious John Brennan was grafting in the fields, James Burrows was drinking ale and gambling at a nearby public house called the Jolly Waggoners, where he was from lunchtime until around 3 p.m. The young Burrows had already met John Brennan during the previous afternoon, when Brennan and he had visited the Jolly Waggoners for a Sunday afternoon pint. Burrows had been gambling and borrowed half a crown from Brennan, but gave it back to him the same day after he had won some money on one of the bets he had placed.

During that Monday afternoon stint in the public house, Burrows again borrowed money, but not from Brennan who was still hard at work in the fields, but from a man named Taylor, also known as 'Germany' for some unstipulated reason. Taylor was the brewer at the Jolly Waggoners and lent Burrows 1s for ale. Henry Clegg, the assistant brewer at nearby Cabbage Hall, Bluepits, was with young James Burrows and both left the inn at 3 p.m. on that Monday afternoon and headed back to the farm, the Jolly Waggoners being situated just up the road from the Hopwood Arms and the Burrows farm.

On nearing the farm, James Burrows asked Henry Clegg to accompany him to Rochdale, asking if he had any money. Clegg replied that he had no money, but said Burrows might be able to 'borrow some from Johnny,' meaning John Brennan, who was still busy with ploughing the nearby field. James Burrows thought this a good idea, as Brennan had lent him quite a considerable sum during the previous afternoon, so he was sure the ploughman would have money on him. Henry Clegg waited on the nearby canal bank, the towpath being the route they would walk along to Rochdale, while James Burrows headed for the field where John Brennan was working. He asked Brennan for the money and Brennan responded by uncoupling the horse from the plough and leading it back to the stable. Henry Clegg watched as Brennan led the horse into the stable, with James Burrows following. Brennan was completely sober, but Burrows was a little unsteady on his feet after all of the ale he had drunk that afternoon.

Henry Clegg grew a little tired of waiting around for James Burrows to return and so headed for the stable in order to see what was delaying his companion. On reaching the stable, Burrows was just coming out. He closed the door behind him. 'Well, how has tha gone on?' asked Henry Clegg. 'He will not find me a bloody ha'penny,' replied Burrows and added, 'Let's go up to Jud's an' we will have a quart of ale.' Jud was the nickname of George Chatburn, the landlord at the Jolly Waggoners.

Isabella Burrows, the sister of James, was still living with her parents at the Hopwood Arms, and during that afternoon her father sent her to feed some calves that were housed in the shippon, which was in the same partitioned building as the stable. This she did and there was nothing untoward that she noticed as she carried out her father's instructions. She later returned to the house, but was immediately asked by her father to go to the stable in order to give the horses hay.

It was by this time about 4 p.m. and Isabella did indeed go to the stable in order to feed the horses. In the process of giving them hay, however, she noticed a man lying on the floor of the stable, parallel with the partition wall which separated the stable from the adjoining shippon (cattle shed). She at first thought that it was Taylor, but soon realised it was her father's new ploughman. She called out 'Johnny,' but he neither moved nor replied to her call. She called out again, but still no answer came, so she looked more closely and was horrified to see that John Brennan's face was covered in blood and that he continued to be still and silent. She ran back to the

'he continued to be still and silent'

inn and told her father that his new employee had been killed. On hearing this, Mr Burrows immediately stopped what he was doing and went to investigate for himself, hoping his daughter was mistaken and that Brennan was still alive.

He quickly discovered, however, that his daughter was correct. John Brennan was indeed dead and had sustained severe injuries about his head. Mr Burrows immediately called in the police and they very quickly established that the 18-year-old James Burrows had been the last person to see John Brennan alive.

Young Burrows was nowhere to be found, however, so the police told his family that they were keen to speak to him and to pass the message on as soon as they saw him. Isabella Burrows went in search of her brother and it seems she knew his habits all too well, as she quickly found him in the Jolly Waggoners, having yet another drink with his friends. He said nothing on hearing the news, but jumped out of his seat and ran out of the inn, heading for the stable. He then went away from the farm and nothing was seen of him until Tuesday when Isabella saw him crossing the road opposite her father's public house. He then headed off towards Thornham Lane shouting to Isabella that he would be 'back in a minute', but she did not see him again until 1 p.m. when he was accompanied by an officer of the law who was walking towards the barn alongside her brother. James Burrows was then arrested and he appeared before Bury magistrates on Thursday, 24 May 1866.

The legal matters involving this case proved to be rather badly organised to begin with, as there was also an inquest held that same Thursday. This meant that James Burrows, appearing before the bench, could not attend the inquest which was held before Mr T.W. Whitehead, the deputy coroner, at the Hopwood Arms, amidst much mystery and intrigue. First of all Whitehead made it clear that accusing fingers must not be pointed at James Burrows, as he was not present to defend himself, which put a bit of a restraint on witnesses and jury alike. A jury of fifteen people listened to witness testimony and much of it put James Burrows on uncomfortable ground, to say the least, though one or two small events during that fateful Monday would surround the case in mystery.

Isabella Burrows had seen the horse John Brennan had been using to plough the field running loose on the road near to the farm at around 3.40 p.m. She asked a lad named Abraham Moore to put the horse back into the stable, which it seems he did, but he obviously failed to see the body of John Brennan lying on the floor, or he kept quiet about the matter if he had which seems unlikely. A lad named Ogden also testified that he had seen the horse running loose. More testimony was given concerning this horse, which was said to have a quiet nature but was newly broken to its work, having only started work on the previous Saturday, the 19 May. The inquest was now beginning to turn away from thoughts of murder and those attending began to think that maybe Brennan had been kicked by the newly broken horse and that it was those injuries that had killed him. This added weight to the importance of the expert medical opinion when Dr Booth of Rochdale was called upon to give testimony.

Booth had carried out the post-mortem on Wednesday afternoon, just the previous day to the inquest, and he gave graphic details regarding his findings. He said that both eyes were discoloured and the mouth was closed, also that the victim's hands were partially clenched. There was a wound an inch long on his right temple, which had penetrated the skull. There was another injury that was over an inch in length and had cut through the frontal region of the skull. A large and deep wound was found on the crown of his head, which had fractured the skull and another wound was found under his left ear. This extended towards the jaw and was very deep, having badly fractured the skull. In the region of this wound Booth found fragments of bone that had pierced the brain and caused injury about the size of half a crown. A smaller wound was found in front of the left ear, with a fracture to the skull here also. There were no other marks or wounds found anywhere and no sign of illness or disease was found when Booth examined the organs. After opening the skull, Booth found that it was much damaged, along with the brain. Death, in his expert opinion, had been caused by the more severe wound under the left ear, where bone fragments had pierced through to the brain.

The jury questioned the doctor and was particularly keen to hear if he thought a horse could have inflicted the injuries to John Brennan's head. Booth was of the opinion that the damage was not consistent with wounds inflicted by a kicking horse. He thought it was much more likely to have been caused by a blunt, heavy instrument and he clearly stated that a common crowbar was a possible weapon.

Mary Ann Clegg, sister of James Burrows and likely the wife of Henry Clegg, stated that her brother had been in the parlour of their home at around 3 p.m. on Monday, 21 May and he had been wearing the shirt produced as evidence. She said she washed it for him on Tuesday afternoon at around 5 p.m. Isabella had put it into the clothes basket for

Burrows and she had seen him with a clean calico shirt on not long after the body had been discovered.

Burrows Snr told of how his daughter had informed him that his ploughman was dead and of how he had run to the stable and seen the body for himself. All testimony ended at this point and two factors meant that the hearing had to be adjourned. Firstly, because James Burrows was not in attendance due to his appearing before magistrates that day, and, secondly, because the jury still could not decide on what had killed John Brennan. They deemed it still possible that the newly broken horse could have inflicted the injuries which killed John Brennan and so the inquest was adjourned until the following week, when young Burrows could attend and more testimony could be heard.

The testimony given the following week would help the jury come to a quick decision regarding this case. The magistrates had remanded Burrows in custody and he was present at the second inquest, which was held at the Queen Ann Inn, Heywood, on Tuesday, 29 May 1866, with Mr Watson representing the accused. This second inquest was attended by large crowds who were spilling out onto the street. A witness came forward at this hearing who had not done so previously, probably because he was a close friend of James Burrows. This was Taylor ('Germany') and what he had to say would completely dispel the possibility of a kicking horse having killed the ploughman.

After James Burrows and Henry Clegg had returned to the Jolly Waggoners, abandoning their previous plans to go to Rochdale, the pair split up, with Burrows going into the brewhouse to see Taylor. This is when Taylor's testimony began. He stated that Burrows asked Taylor if he could wash and Taylor noticed that Burrows had blood spatter on his tie and collar, which Burrows quickly took off and put into the furnace to burn. Taylor then told of how Burrows paid back the shilling he had borrowed that very morning, which suggests that Burrows had somehow obtained money as he had nothing on him at 3 p.m., nor when he had been compelled to ask Henry Clegg and then John Brennan for money to go to Rochdale. The jury must have by now suspected that Burrows had committed armed robbery against John Brennan. Such suspicions would be verified by what Taylor next told the hearing.

He said that Burrows, after burning his collar and tie and paying back the shilling he owed, told him straight that 'I have killed yon Brennan in the stable.' Taylor replied, 'I'm sure you have never killed him.' Young Burrows then said, 'I have.' 'What have you killed him with?' asked Taylor. 'With a crowbar,' was the reply. Taylor then testified that he had said to Burrows, 'You will be found out Jem,' to which he replied, 'Not if they cannot find the bar. I put it in a hole in a wall and they will have to pull it down to find it.' It seems that Burrows did not say which wall, but it was likely a drystone wall somewhere on, or near, his father's farm.

James Burrows then asked Taylor to take part in a sham fight with him and to burst his nose, presumably in an effort to explain away the blood spatter on his clothing. They went into a field next to the Jolly Waggoners and there had the sham fight, which witnesses testified was fooling no one. They said that the fight was obviously staged, as the pair were not hitting each other properly. In fact, some witnesses said that Burrows never struck Taylor at all. However, Taylor did carry out James Burrows' wishes by busting his nose, which had the desired effect of spattering blood about his person. Taylor's evidence was a revelation at this second inquest and the jury was now no longer considering the possibility that the newly broken working horse had accidentally killed Brennan by kicking him in the head.

It took a very short time for a verdict to be reached and James Burrows was found guilty of willful murder. The magistrates considered the findings of the inquest and agreed, committing James Burrows for trial at the New Bailey, Salford. Burrows was then moved from his cell at Bury Police Station where he had been held on remand since his arrest on 22 May, to the New Bailey at Salford on 1 June 1866, to await trial.

The trial was held on 3 August 1866 and the accused was defended by Mr Torr, while Mr Holker and Mr Addison stood for the prosecution. Mr Holker opened the proceedings and described the case against the prisoner, stating that James Burrows had been charged with willful murder, bringing out what reporters at the time described as the 'dreadful character of the crime committed against John Brennan'. He also told the court that John Brennan had only started working for Burrows Snr on the very day that he was so viciously and cruelly murdered, and all for the lowly amount of money that his killer wanted for the purchasing of ale. The prosecution made it clear to the court and the jury in particular, that James Burrows, who sat through his trial with complete indifference, was one of life's wastrels: a drunkard and gambler who could neither read nor write and who spent most of his time avoiding work and sleeping in barns and stables.

The prosecution also brought out the plight of John Brennan, a hard-working farm labourer doing his utmost to provide for his wife and six children, who were now left widowed and fatherless. Mr Holker then described the scene of the events of that day, being of the opinion that it would help the jury if he described the situation of the farm and the inns involved in this horrific and terrible case.

The Hopwood Arms was situated on the side of the Manchester to Rochdale road and the land farmed by the publican, Mr Burrows, was all around the inn. Opposite the Hopwood Arms was the turnpike road and the towpath of the canal, more farmland owned by Mr Burrows and the farm and its buildings. On the right side of the farm was the building that housed both the stable and shippon.

After this the case progressed and all witnesses involved were heard, their testimony pretty damning to the accused who showed such indifference throughout that it was reported that James Burrows 'did not seem aware of his sad situation'. It was said that he maintained a cold, hardened and unemotional aspect through the whole of the proceedings.

The jury heard all of the testimony at the trial and retired to consider their verdict. It did not take long. Especially authoritative was the testimony of Dr Booth that a horse was very unlikely to have caused such injuries and that a crowbar was the most likely weapon used to kill the victim. This, coupled with Taylor's testimony that Burrows had confessed to the killing in his presence on the very afternoon that the murder took place, not to mention the blood seen on his clothes, was convincing evidence to say the least. The jury was soon back in court and the verdict was read out.

James Burrows was found guilty of the willful murder of John Brennan, but the jury asked that Burrows be shown mercy because of his youthfulness and the evil ways he had fallen into. The judge, however, did not agree. He passed the death sentence and young Burrows was led from the dock and taken back to his prison cell at the New Bailey.

The date of the hanging was set for 18 August 1866, but the justice system found itself unprepared for the occasion. This was to be the first execution staged in Manchester, as hangings were previously carried out at Kirkdale, so the date was postponed for a short time. It was reported that after the verdict was read out and the sentence passed, Burrows changed his previously cold, hardened and indifferent attitude. He began to welcome visits by the prison chaplain, Mr C.F. Bagshaw and Mr Wright, who was at that time reported as a 'well known philanthropist'. Burrows learnt to read to some extent while awaiting execution and he became particularly fond of Psalm 51, which deals with King David's penitence after sinning against God with Bathsheba and arranging for her husband to be killed in battle in order that he could take her for himself. Burrows became penitent too, learning Psalm 51 by heart in the short time between sentence being passed and the day of his execution. Burrows also expressed great concern for the widow and children of John Brennan, regretting bitterly that he could do nothing to help them, saying to the prison chaplain that he 'had nothing to leave them'. In the meantime, letters and petitions were sent to the Home Secretary appealing for a reprieve and for the sentence of a lifetime of penal servitude to be passed instead, but the Home Secretary was unmoved. After all, Burrows had willfully and viciously murdered John Brennan for the sake of a few pennies and such actions deserved the full penalty of the law. And so preparations for the hanging continued apace and the scene was set for the new date of Burrows' execution, which was to take place on Saturday, 25 August 1866.

Several sites for the occasion had been proposed, looked over and dismissed as unsuitable, mostly because large crowds were expected to attend due to the horrific nature of the crime, the youthfulness of the perpetrator and the uniqueness of the occasion, this being the first execution to be staged in Manchester. The New Bailey was finally settled on as the most suitable venue under the circumstances. Scaffold was erected around the execution site and in adjoining streets from Salford railway station right up to Bridge Street, in order to provide visiting folk with a decent view. This was going to be a big occasion and preparations for the execution, much more than the trial itself, attracted huge media attention as newspapers kept their readers informed throughout the country.

Unbelievably, people began gathering on the morning of Friday, 24 August and started taking up their positions for the hanging even before the erection of the scaffolding had been completed; the huge task was finally finished at noon that day. People were arriving from towns and villages from several miles away, as well as more local Manchester districts, and it wasn't long before numbers were reaching into the thousands. Many watched as William Calcraft, the appointed hangman, supervised the erecting of the gallows.

A party atmosphere soon pervaded the streets around the execution site and local businesses, it was reported at the time, did a roaring trade, especially the local inns where drinking and gambling went on late into Friday evening. Believe it or not, folk actually laid bets on Burrows' demeanour when he looked death in the face on those gallows come Saturday morning. After the drinking and gambling had finally finished, people camped out at any convenient place they could find that would afford a decent view on the morrow and there they slept for the night, waking the next morning with sore heads no doubt and just in time to begin witnessing one of the largest gatherings that has ever taken place.

Newspapers reported that over 70,000 people gathered during that Saturday morning, filling streets and scaffolding round about the New Bailey, right along Chapel Street (made famous a few decades later in *Hobson's Choice*, the incredibly popular play and novel written by Harold Brighouse), towards Pendleton and up Bridge Street as far as the

London Music Hall. Calcraft appeared at the gallows later that morning and he was greeted with shouting and cheers from the huge crowds filling the streets around the New Bailey as far as the eye could see. They were there to see a hanging and they knew that Calcraft was their man.

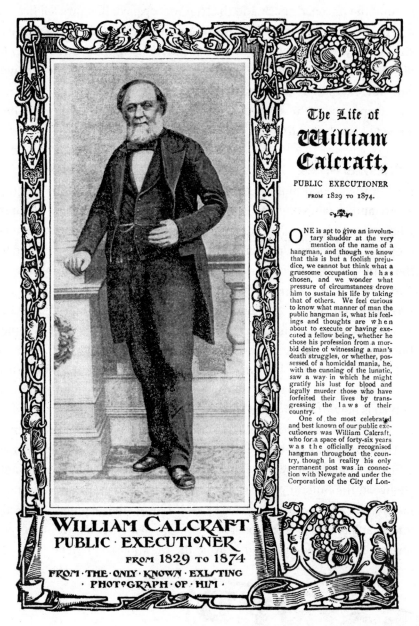

The Life of

William Calcraft,

PUBLIC EXECUTIONER
FROM 1829 TO 1874.

ONE is apt to give an involuntary shudder at the very mention of the name of a hangman, and though we know that this is but a foolish prejudice, we cannot but think what a gruesome occupation he has chosen, and we wonder what pressure of circumstances drove him to sustain his life by taking that of others. We feel curious to know what manner of man the public hangman is, what his feelings and thoughts are when about to execute or having executed a fellow being, whether he chose his profession from a morbid desire of witnessing a man's death struggles, or whether, possessed of a homicidal mania, he, with the cunning of the lunatic, saw a way in which he might gratify his lust for blood and legally murder those who have forfeited their lives by transgressing the laws of their country.

One of the most celebrated and best known of our public executioners was William Calcraft, who for a space of forty-six years was the officially recognised hangman throughout the country, though in reality his only permanent post was in connection with Newgate and under the Corporation of the City of Lon-

WILLIAM CALCRAFT
PUBLIC · EXECUTIONER ·
FROM 1829 TO 1874
FROM · THE · ONLY · KNOWN · EXISTING ·
· PHOTOGRAPH · OF · HIM ·

James Burrows, to his credit and as a sign of his penitence, provided a written confession before he was hanged and shortly after Calcraft arrived on the scaffold. Burrows appeared, the crowd eagerly watching his demeanour and hoping to win their bets. Calcraft placed the noose around the prisoner's neck and the trap was opened. Burrows fell heavily and death, it was reported by eyewitnesses, was very quick, as the prisoner struggled very little. Immediately after the hanging the crowds began to disperse, though some did wait around in order to see the body cut down. Not long after James Burrows was dead, the once packed and lively streets were empty and silent, as though folk had never gathered there. Justice had come to Manchester that day.

Additional Notes:

During the second inquest into the murder of John Brennan, the jury showed great sympathy towards the grieving widow and her six children who, it was said, were now sadly heading for the workhouse. And so the jury proposed a public subscription in order to help out the family left behind by the hard-working and conscientious ploughman and general farm worker. The public quickly responded and almost immediately the sum of £6 15s was raised, an amount that had increased to a very handsome £12 by the end of the inquest, which had by that time established the guilt of James Burrows and the tragic and violent end to the life of a family man.

John Brennan was buried a few days after the inquest and a grave was prepared in the pauper's burial ground at Bury Workhouse, Jericho (which is now where Fairfield Hospital is situated), the site being owned by the Bury Union. Mr Brown provided the coffin and arranged the funeral.

The corpse was borne to its final resting place in a shillibeer hearse, which was followed by only four people. However, on passing through Heywood the funeral procession attracted a lot of attention from local people. The service was conducted by Mr F. Wilson, the incumbent of Birtle and chaplain to the workhouse. It is not known whether Mrs Brennan and her six children managed to avoid the workhouse at Jericho.

CASE THREE   1887

A FRENZIED ATTACK

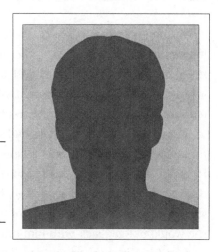

Suspect:	Walter Wood
Age:	?
Charge:	Murder

A woman lay dead in the doorway of a dairy at a Bury farm and a police hunt was now well under way in order to catch the murderer. The victim was 30-year-old Emma Wood and the suspected murderer was her husband, Walter Wood, who was an engine fitter by trade but who had been out of work for some time previous to this incident. The police came very close to catching Walter Wood in Bolton, but it later transpired that he had got into a pond in a public park and hid from his pursuers there. However, on returning to his mother's house in Bolton, the police seized and arrested him. The date was Thursday, 17 February 1887 and the murder had taken place that very afternoon.

Problems had mounted in the marriage of Walter and Emma Wood after he lost regular employment and had taken to drinking far too frequently and with money that should have been spent on necessary things, like food and clothing. It all got a little too much for Emma Wood and towards the back end of 1886 she had finally left her husband, who continued to show more enthusiasm for local pubs than he did for seeking work. She went to live with her brother and sister-in-law in Clarendon Street in Freetown near Walmersley, while Walter Wood eventually moved back in with his mother in Bolton after losing their home; no doubt the rent money was spent on beer instead. While estranged from his wife, Wood continued to frequent local inns. He also pestered Emma to get back with him, but she refused, alluding to his drinking and lack of employment as the basic problems in their marriage.

Walter arranged to see his wife in January at the home of her brother and sister-in-law in Clarendon Street and it proved to be a meeting fraught with tension. The meeting could have resulted in Emma Wood being terrified, had she taken her husband's threats seriously. He asked her to return to him so that they could resume their marriage, but she once again refused, telling him that she would not get back with him unless he found steady employment and settled down to married life.

An area near the bottom of Walmersley Road frequented by Walter Wood as he drank the hours away.

He did not take this news well, crashing his fist down on the kitchen table and telling her in his rage that her decision could prove fatal. She laughed at this remark, but he then went on to tell her that if she did not get back with him he would kill her, warning his wife not to take his threats lightly. These threats were heard by Frederick Ford, the brother of Emma Wood, who would later testify at the inquest before the Bury Police Court and before the Manchester Assizes when the case came to trial. The account did not state if Mr Ford intervened at this point, but it seems likely, as the meeting between the estranged couple now ended.

On Thursday, 17 February 1887 Walter Wood approached a boy in the street named John Edward Smith and gave him a letter, asking him to take the correspondence round to Clarendon Street and to give it to Emma Wood. The letter was basically asking Emma Wood to meet him opposite the General Washington Inn on Walmersley Road. Emma Wood did not answer after the boy had knocked at the door of the house in Clarendon Street, but Elizabeth Ellen Ford did. She was the illegitimate daughter of Emma Wood, from a previous relationship. She passed the letter to her mother and it read: 'The person you call Walter Wood [he wrote this because he was also known as Rueben Wood] is waiting to see you beside Fitton's beerhouse, Walmersley Road. Come on, as I have got a good place of work and have no time to wait – Walter Wood.'

After reading the letter, Emma Wood said to her daughter that she feared this would mean more trouble, but went to meet him anyway. Elizabeth later saw her mother and Walter Wood walking away together. During that afternoon there were several sightings of the pair around Bury. Thomas Olive, a labourer who resided at Chesham Place, which is maybe a 10 minute walk east of Walmersley Road, later saw them heading towards Heap Bridge at around 3 p.m., via the Bridge Hall Mills district which was at one time a heavily industrialised part of Bury.

Robert Ashworth, a carter by trade, also saw them that afternoon at around 3.30 p.m. as they walked together in the direction of Emerson's Farm which was situated in the Huntley Brook area of Bury. The farm is now long gone and the footpath where they walked, known as Wrigley's footpath, is now likely built upon. It would seem that Emma Wood was making her way back to Freetown and Clarendon Street, but unfortunately she would not make it home. Walter Wood would make certain of that, as he pestered her to return to him, while she continued to refuse. It may well be that he had lied about having secured employment in order to get her to meet him. Emma Wood had been right about there being more trouble to come.

Joseph Emerson of Huntley Brook Farm saw them that afternoon too, as they walked towards his farm, so it is likely that the time would have been around the same, or a little after, as that reported by Robert Ashworth. A few minutes after this sighting, a little girl came running to Joseph Emerson and told him that a man had cut a woman's throat. He then went to his farm and there found the body of poor Emma Wood lying in the doorway of his dairy, with a large pool of blood around her. Emerson would later testify that her throat had been cut 'from ear to ear'. It was

Walmersley Road today.

31

a gruesome discovery that marked the culmination of a frenzied attack by the husband of Emma Wood, though he would plead not guilty when up before the inquest, the magistrates at the Bury Police Court, and the Manchester Assizes.

'her throat had been cut "from ear to ear"'

An inquest was held on Monday, 21 February at the Bridge Inn, Freetown and there Walter Wood was found guilty of willful murder. He then appeared before magistrates at the Bury Police Court on Monday, 28 February 1887 on a charge of the willful murder of his wife. The magistrates were Mr J. O'Neill, Alderman Hall and Mr T. Cornall. The prisoner was defended by Mr P. Marsh of Bolton and standing for the prosecution was Superintendent Henderson. The magistrates, having heard the several witnesses who could testify to Walter Wood having been the last person seen with Emma Wood on Thursday, 17 February 1887, and that he was seen with her only moments before she died, decided that Walter Wood had a case to answer and so he was committed for trial at the Manchester Assizes.

The Huntley Brook area today. The farm is now long gone.

The trial date was set for Monday, 9 May 1887 before Justice Wills and Mr McKeand stood for the defense, while Mr Foard and H. M. Hamilton stood for the prosecution. Wood pleaded not guilty yet again, but the testimony of the witnesses who appeared would soon build a damning case against him, which sorely tried the abilities of the defense.

Frederick Ford told of how Walter Wood had threatened to kill Emma Wood when visiting her at his home in January. Elizabeth Ellen Ford told of how she had been given the letter, which she had passed to her mother. Thomas Olive and Robert Ashworth told of how they had seen the pair together on that fateful afternoon, and Joseph Emerson told of his sighting of them and of how he had come upon the dead woman only moments later. But even more damning evidence was to be heard at the trial that day.

Mrs Jane Kay appeared as a witness for the prosecution and she told of her harrowing experiences that afternoon. Mrs Kay lived with her husband in a cottage at the farm and Emma Wood came running towards her, telling her that her husband had cut her throat on Wrigley's footpath. Mrs Kay then assisted the victim into the doorway of the dairy and a doctor was sent for. Mrs Kay stated that she did not take Emma to her cottage because her husband was ill at the time (though the amount of blood spilling from the victim may have had something to do with it!). Mrs Farrar was passing at the time and she helped, going for the doctor while Mrs Kay attempted to stop the bleeding, which she described as pumping out 'like a fountain' by this time. The doctor arrived very quickly, but he was too late. She died only a minute or two after his arrival. The doctor stated that a razor or a very sharp knife had inflicted the fatal wound. Before dying she had managed to tell the doctor that her husband had cut her throat. The police arrived shortly afterwards and a manhunt began immediately, but Wood managed to evade capture until reaching his home at Thynne Street in Bolton, where he was finally apprehended and arrested by Sergeant Thomas Miller of the Bolton Police, who later handed over the prisoner to their colleagues in Bury.

The evidence against Walter Wood proved so damning that the jury only deliberated for 3 or 4 minutes before finding him 'guilty of willful murder'. Justice Wills then passed the death sentence, as the jury had recommended that no mercy be shown to the prisoner. The execution date was set for Monday, 30 May 1887 and Walter Wood was said to have shown very little

The route the killer took back to Freetown.

emotion when the death sentence was passed. A reprieve was sought by a few supporters of Walter Wood, but the Home Office remained unmoved by pleas for mercy and Walter Wood was hanged with little ceremony at Manchester on Monday, 30 May as arranged.

Additional Notes:

Although he showed little emotion when hearing the death sentence passed by Justice Wills who was donned in his fearsome black cap for the occasion, it was reported that Walter Wood afterwards became greatly depressed. He stated that he had no intention of killing his wife, but that she had reproached him so much for his past conduct that he lost his temper, going into a frenzy and losing control of himself.

He heard of the attempts to obtain a reprieve and subsequently knew that they were unsuccessful, so just wanted the day of his execution to hurry. It was said that Wood did become penitent, but all of the evidence led to just one conclusion; Walter Wood had planned to kill his wife if she would not get back together with him. His threats had been clearly heard and so the sentence of death and the eventual execution could be the only satisfactory outcome to this dreadful crime. Justice at last caught up with Walter Wood.

A MURDER OF TREMENDOUS VIOLENCE

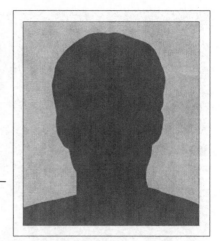

Suspect:	William Dukes
Age:	?
Charge:	Murder

Samuel Gordon received a telegram from his son on Wednesday, 25 September 1889 and the contents immediately aroused his suspicion. The telegram stated: 'Gone to Burnley: return tomorrow: all right – George.' This apparently innocent telegram was so out of character and different to the plans for the day that George Gordon had discussed with his father, that Samuel couldn't help but be suspicious and more than a little worried about his son's whereabouts.

George's plans had been to meet William Dukes, the manager of the Gordon furniture shop in Bolton Street, Bury, at their head office in Manchester, to discuss discrepancies in the accounts book. However, Dukes hadn't put in an appearance and so Gordon had gone to Bury in order to confront his shop manager about the accounts that were his responsibility to keep in proper order.

George Gordon had not returned to Manchester on the Thursday morning and so Samuel Gordon and his other son Meyer, George's brother, headed for Bury and went to the police station there to report their missing relative. The police were very reluctant to help and a frustrated Samuel Gordon told them that his son could only be kept away from his business by death. Gordon was adamant that something terrible had happened and so the police eventually, though still rather reluctantly, agreed to make enquiries. They accompanied Samuel and Meyer Gordon to the Bury shop at No. 39 Bolton Street and there began a search of the premises.

A veterinary surgery not far from Gordon's furniture shop.

William Dukes was at the shop and he insisted that George Gordon had indeed gone to Burnley, accompanied by a woman. However, the father and brother did not believe his unlikely tale and very soon a number of clues as to what had really occurred began to surface, rousing suspicions even among the police as a consequence. First of all, when they searched the cellar they found a small area of the ground had been dug up for a few inches of depth, but solid ground below meant that whoever had begun digging there had soon given up. Suspicious marks were also found on a hearth and a boiler in one of the rooms; despite them being freshly whitewashed what looked like bloodstains were just visible in places.

Even so, when a locked wardrobe was found upstairs with the lock freshly fitted, the police were reluctant to open it despite the owner of the shop insisting that they did. They were especially reluctant after William Dukes told them that a woman from Rochdale had bought the wardrobe and that it was she who had had the lock fitted. He also told them that he had arranged for delivery that same day.

If it wasn't for the fuss Samuel and Meyer Gordon kicked up, it is unlikely the police would have bothered to look in that wardrobe at all. They seemed to believe every word Dukes said, despite so much evidence around them that something sinister had very recently occurred in the shop. Samuel and Meyer were so insistent that eventually the police did wrench off the lock and there they discovered the body of George Gordon, wrapped in flocks bags, a hearth rug, a towel and a piece of cloth. A hammer and a small pickaxe were also found lying next to the body in the wardrobe. Meyer Gordon shouted, 'He is here, you murderer,' directing his charge at William Dukes, and immediately Dukes turned to the police

'He is here, you murderer'

and said, 'Well, I have done it. I will tell you all about it.' He was then led away to the police station and it was a little later, at the inquest, that the truth of what had occurred during the previous day finally came out.

William Dukes appeared before the bench at the Bury Police Court on 27 September 1889 and was charged with willful murder and remanded in custody at Strangeways Gaol in Manchester. An inquest into the death of George Gordon was held in Bury from Wednesday, 2 October to Friday, 4 October 1889, before the district coroner, Mr Butcher. It was here that all of the details of what later would be described as 'a murder of tremendous violence' would be heard, before a packed assembly.

George Gordon's business details were first heard. He was a partner in his father's furniture shop business, with branches in Manchester and Bury. There had been some bad blood between Gordon and William Dukes for a number of weeks, because discrepancies had been found in the accounts book. Gordon had arranged a number of meetings between himself and Dukes, in order to sort out this matter, but Dukes had come up with all kinds of fake appointments in an attempt to avoid the issue. Another matter that had been worrying Gordon was the increased drinking of Dukes, who had been supping in Bury alehouses during working hours. In fact, Dukes' father had also become worried about his son's drinking problem, which had begun to affect his marriage. The press reported that Dukes had become abusive to his wife and had recently threatened to

'Jack the Ripper' her, but she denied such allegations. The father and two sisters of William Dukes lived at No. 105 Turton Road, Bradshaw, and all had been very disturbed to hear about the terrible murder.

Dukes was originally a native of Burton-on-Trent, but had later moved north where he had married a Miss Kershaw, the daughter of a schoolmaster in Manchester Road, Bolton, and they had settled in Paradise Street, Bury. Despite a seemingly good start, the marriage had eventually turned sour after Dukes had begun drinking too much, a bad habit that quickly put a serious strain on their relationship. There was no proof, but it seemed that Dukes had become violent towards his wife, at least in speech, but whether or not that had spilled over into physical violence was not known, neither could such facts be ascertained.

When Dukes senior had expressed his concerns about his son's increased drinking habits, his daughter-in-law had dismissed such concerns, as though her husband's drinking wasn't a problem. However, his drinking habit had become so addictive he began stealing money from the Gordon furniture shop in Bury in order to fund it. He then attempted to avoid the consequences when confronted about the accounts by George Gordon.

Dr Mitchell stated his findings, saying that he had found blood on the trousers of William Dukes. He also said there were several wounds on the body of George Gordon, one a quarter of an inch long. He found blood on a hearthstone, a skirting leading to the cellar, a quarryman's hammer and a screwdriver. The doctor was of the opinion that the hammer had caused the worst of the wounds. Dr Jones corroborated this testimony. At hearing this evidence, Samuel Gordon broke down and wept bitterly.

George Fowler of Manchester also gave evidence. He was a carter by trade and often took furniture from Manchester to the store in Bury, as well as carrying out deliveries from the Bury shop to local residencies. He stated that on that fateful Wednesday he transported furniture goods from Manchester to Bury and while waiting for the manager, William Dukes, to deal with him, he heard George Gordon speaking to Dukes in 'a loud and angry tone'. A little later, Dukes approached Fowler and told him that Gordon had gone to Prestwich and that he must take some goods to a house in that town. William Toothill, a boy working at the Bury shop, was also sent along to assist Fowler, but on searching throughout the Prestwich area they could not find the address Dukes had supplied. It later became obvious that Dukes had sent the pair on a wild goose chase in order to get them out of the way for a few hours, creating a fictitious Mr Halstead as the purchaser of the goods. Fowler later returned to Bury and William Dukes told him, 'If Mr Gordon asks about his son, he has gone to Burnley.' Fowler then made the return journey to Manchester. Where young Toothill was at this time is unclear, because when he returned to the shop it was all locked up.

Inspector McQueen gave evidence, as he had been in charge of the search at the Bury furniture shop. The body of George Gordon was found on Thursday, 26 September, but the premises continued to be investigated until the Saturday of that week. The inspector confirmed that blood had been found on the premises and that there had been a very recent attempted dig in the cellar. The inspector was unable to determine exactly where William Dukes went after committing the alleged murder on the Wednesday, but a light was seen at his house in Paradise Street at around 1 a.m.

He also stated that witnesses had seen Dukes drinking in Bury alehouses on the Wednesday and Thursday. In fact, a friend of Dukes told the police that he had been drinking with the accused during that Wednesday afternoon and Dukes' hands were shaking as he held his glass. He also said that Dukes had sent a telegram, which would have been the one received by Samuel Gordon, stating that his son had gone to Burnley. Dukes must have been drinking at lunchtime on the Thursday too, as he was arrested that afternoon when the body was finally discovered by Constables Bremner and McClelland, who had also helped in the search.

The inspector also said William Dukes had told him that he had given George Gordon £5 10s towards the monies missing in the accounts, but not a penny was found on the body. He also told the packed hearing that only Dukes' father had visited him in prison and his wife could not bring herself to do so. William Dukes had been taken to Strangeways Gaol in Manchester by train and was walked from Victoria Station to the prison grounds, guarded by officers, as a large crowd assembled and began 'hooting' at the prisoner.

The wife of the accused had been in a very bad state since her husband's crime became known. It was said she was hysterical and unable to speak to anyone, though in calmer moments she did state that her husband had not threatened her. However, Inspector McQueen said that on Wednesday, the same day as George Gordon's murder, Dukes had sent for his wife by telegram and had asked her to 'come by last train'. She had been staying with a relative, but was too ill to return home that night. Had she done so, it was thought that she too would have been murdered. This speculation had greatly unsettled Mrs Dukes, as well as the awful murder of her husband's employer (reading between the lines, it seems the police suspected that Dukes had planned to murder his wife and then claim she had run away to Burnley with George Gordon).

William Dukes admitted to the police that he had killed Gordon, but claimed he had acted in self-defense. This meant the question to be settled was whether this had been a willful, premeditated murder or manslaughter. Dukes claimed that Gordon was known for his hot temper and that he attacked him while discussing the accounts; Dukes defended himself and accidentally killed his employer whilst doing so. He then panicked and tried to hide the body. He had first attempted to dig a hole in the cellar, but could not due to the hard ground, so had decided to put the body in a wardrobe and remove it later for disposal elsewhere. However, a witness gave evidence that Dukes had bought the pickaxe in town on the Tuesday evening of 24 September. The boy, Toothill also gave evidence that he had helped Dukes carry the wardrobe and fit a lock on the morning of the murder. He also stated that he had seen Dukes burning some books, which he thought were account books, a few days earlier. It took just 15 minutes for the decision of willful murder to be reached and William Dukes was then committed for trial at the Manchester Assizes. The trial date was set for 4 December 1889.

The trial of William Dukes at Manchester Assizes was heard before Justice Charles. Mr Blair and Mr Parry appeared for the prosecution, while Mr Cottingham appeared for the defense. It was heard how the victim had been a partner in his father's furniture shop business and that George Gordon attended the Bury shop in Bolton Street every Tuesday in order to look over the accounts. The court heard how William Dukes had put off the last three Tuesday appointments in an effort to avoid facing questions about certain discrepancies in the accounts, which suggested fraudulent actions by the accused.

After Dukes had dodged yet more appointments at Manchester, George Gordon decided to go to the shop at Bury in order to confront his shop manager about the accounts, but was forced to wait around as Dukes was in the pub at lunchtime. Fowler and Toothill were sent away from the shop by Dukes and that was the last time Gordon was seen alive. He had been engaged in a lively discussion with William Dukes, just before the manager had sent his staff to Prestwich on a fictitious delivery.

All the medical evidence was heard and the experts stated that the injuries were caused mostly by a hammer, with blood found on the screwdriver that was also used to inflict injury. The prosecution put the case forward that George Gordon was examining the accounts when William Dukes lunged at him with the quarryman's hammer found at the scene, and hit him with it repeatedly. He then grabbed a screwdriver and stabbed him with it. Blood found at the scene along the skirting suggested that Gordon's body had been dragged. It seems Dukes had tried to dig a hole in the cellar the previous evening, but had quickly realised that the ground was just too hard to effect a deep enough hole, so he gave up on that idea and had young Toothill help him to fit a lock on a wardrobe the following morning, the day of the murder. Dukes had planned to hide the body in the wardrobe until he could move and dispose of it when he got the opportunity.

William Dukes heard all of this evidence and later gave a statement to the packed courtroom. He said that George Gordon, known for having a hot temper according to Dukes, attacked him, so he was left with no choice but to defend himself. He said that, due to the drink he had imbibed at lunchtime, as well as the passion he got himself into, he could remember very little of the incident, but afterwards feared for his life and that is why he had tried to cover up what he had done. This testimony from the killer caused a sensation in court, but the evidence was stacked against the accused.

There was little sympathy from the prosecution, who quickly brought out several facts that pointed to this being a premeditated murder of 'tremendous violence'. The pickaxe had been bought the evening before the murder and the cellar had been dug, but the hard ground had put paid to that option of disposing of the body. The wardrobe had also been placed in an out-of-the-way area and had been fitted with a lock before the murder took place. Dukes had also sent his staff away on a bogus delivery. He couldn't face his boss over the missing monies betrayed by the accounts, so killed him instead in order to attempt to cover up his 'deceit and fraud' as the prosecution put it. On hearing all of this weighty testimony, the prisoner wept with a bowed head.

The defense had been attempting to reduce the charge to manslaughter, but the judge was not impressed and the compelling evidence of the prosecution quickly brought a reaction from Justice Charles. He stated decisively that he would not reduce the charge to that of manslaughter. The jury then took their leave to deliberate and returned a verdict of 'guilty of willful murder'. William Dukes then received the death sentence from the stern judge and was led away to the condemned cell at Strangeways Gaol. There he awaited his fate.

Even though William Dukes had been found guilty of a murder of tremendous violence, with all of the evidence proving beyond any reasonable doubt that he had committed a premeditated act, there were still supporters who attempted to get a reprieve for him. However, the Home Secretary, after carefully considering the case, came to the conclusion that there were no grounds for a reprieve. And so Dukes remained in the condemned cell and his final night was a depressed and restless one. Dukes ate a good breakfast early that morning, on Tuesday, 24 December 1889, and the prison chaplain was with him till just before 8 a.m. He was then led out to the yard and was pinioned by Mr Berry. Members of the press were in attendance at the place of execution and William Dukes asked them to 'tell my wife that I die happy'. The bolt was then drawn and it was reported that the murderer died immediately. I doubt poor George Gordon received such a quick ending to his life!

Additional Notes:

The funeral of George Gordon was held on Sunday, 29 September 1889 at the Hebrew cemetery in Manchester, with large crowds attending. The body was conveyed to Manchester after sunset on Saturday, 28 September, once the Sabbath had ended. It was reported that thousands of mourners turned out to support the family and to pay their last respects to Gordon, who was a popular member of the Cheetham synagogue. Permission had been sought by the family to bury Gordon in the clothes in which he died, but the coroner had reluctantly refused such permission, due to the ongoing nature of investigations and the forthcoming inquest. The clothes were needed as evidence, as they were covered in blood.

Dr Solomon, the minister of the Great Synagogue, Manchester, which George Gordon had attended with his family, stated to the gathered mourners that Gordon had been murdered 'at the hand of a villain, by a brute'. He also brought out that this was not a crime of religious hatred (there may have been some fear among the Jewish community that religious hatred may have been behind this murder, but there was no evidence to suggest that), but that murder had been committed by a man who 'had debased himself with drunkenness and deceit'. The funeral of the victim was truly a sad occasion. The savage murder of George Gordon had affected a wide-ranging community and that was reflected in the numbers who attended on that mournful day.

CASE FIVE   1900

MURDER?

Suspect: James Partington
Age: ?
Charge: Murder

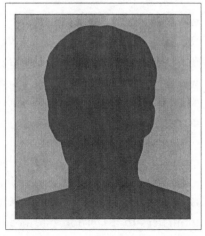

James Partington and Thomas Entwistle spent the evening of Wednesday, 1 August 1900 in the parlour of the Hare & Hounds at Holcombe Brook, where they became friends during a very agreeable sojourn at the inn. Annie Yates was the landlady at the time and she enjoyed their company that evening, later stating that Partington was an amiable and sociable man who was also usually sober in his habits. The two men each bought a half-pint of neat whisky towards closing time and headed off to nearby High Ridge Farm, which belonged to Partington, in order to continue their social jollities. What happened then became a matter of great controversy and the exact truth remains a mystery to this day, for only Partington knew what really occurred during that night and he took the truth with him to the grave.

Thomas Entwistle was from Pendleton, a district of Manchester, and what he was doing in Bury was not recorded. He may have been in the town on business or perhaps seeking work in the Bury area. Whatever the reason for visiting the town, he soon made friends with Partington and it was a meeting he would very quickly regret.

'it was a meeting he would very quickly regret'

At 2 a.m. on 2 August 1900, John Knowles of Higher Ridge Farm was woken by a furious knocking at his front door. It was James Partington in a distressed state, exclaiming that he had 'killed a man'. Knowles then woke his neighbour Henry Livesey and both made for High Ridge Farm in order to investigate Partington's outrageous and unlikely claims. There, to their horror, they discovered the lifeless body of Thomas Entwistle lying in a pool of his own blood at the bottom of the stairs. The police were called in immediately and James Partington was arrested and held in custody until the events of that night could be properly ascertained.

Constable Wilson and Sergeant Thickett arrived at the scene and Constable Wilson later described how he found the body of Thomas Entwistle lying in a pool of blood at the foot of the stairs, just as John Knowles and Henry Livesey had done earlier that night. Sergeant Thickett was the arresting officer and when he arrived on the scene he asked Partington to bring him the garment he was wearing at the time, which was his night attire, and discovered that the right sleeve was covered in blood. James Partington had one sound arm, the right being partly severed with a stump and a crook fitted. The fitting for the crook also had bloodstains on it. Sergeant Thickett then told Partington that he would be facing a charge of willful murder, but Partington replied, 'No, what I did I was justified in doing.'

The Hare & Hounds today, which has changed little since James Partington and Thomas Entwistle drank together here on that fateful evening.

The police also discovered two whisky bottles at the scene, one empty and the other ⅔ full, and a broken jug lying on the floor. But the events of that fateful night were not very clear at all, as James Partington, the only one who really knew what had occurred, seemed fuddled and confused and was unclear in his explanations. Reading between the lines, however, it seems the police were convinced that a willful murder had occurred and that Partington was guilty of such a serious crime. Partington was remanded in custody until an inquest was held at the end of the following week, where he appeared to give evidence, guarded by the police of course.

The inquest was held at the Royal Hotel in Silver Street, Bury, and John Knowles was the first to give evidence. He told the packed hearing of the events which had occurred during the early hours of 2 August, when James Partington had knocked him awake at 2 a.m., and of how he and Henry Livesey had gone to High Ridge Farm where they found the dead body of Thomas Entwistle. There was nothing in John Knowles' testimony to suggest that Partington believed he had accidentally killed Entwistle, for it seems that Partington did not make such a claim at any time during the proceedings. Annie Yates of the Hare & Hounds inn gave her evidence too, which was favourable towards the accused. Sergeant Thickett also gave his testimony and the police were obviously hoping for a charge of willful murder, but the expert evidence of Dr Mitchell was yet to be heard at the inquest and this would surely be pivotal in providing the jury with a verdict.

Sergeant Thickett told the hearing that James Partington had denied willful murder, exclaiming that he was justified in his actions, but still nothing was said about this being an accident. This suggests Partington himself believed that he had killed Entwistle by hitting him about the head with his stump, and that he had good reason for such actions. But would the medical evidence provide what the police needed to get the verdict they wanted?

Dr Mitchell took his place before the inquest at the Royal Hotel, the pervading mixed scents of ale and spirits all around the gloomy interior, and he first stated that he had never before come across a skull like that of Thomas Entwistle's. 'His skull is the thinnest I have ever seen on a man,' he told Mr Butcher, the district coroner overseeing the inquest, and then he reported his findings stating that Entwistle died 'due to a contusion of the brain'. He had carried out a thorough examination of the body and had found no evidence of disease, or any other complaint that could have resulted in death. The thinness of the skull, together with the severe head injuries he had sustained, was the cause of his death. This testimony must have greatly encouraged the police.

James Partington had already told his version of events during the early hours of that Thursday morning. He claimed that he thought Thomas Entwistle was an imposter who had made friends with him in order to get into his home and, once there, rob him. He explained how he and his new friend had enjoyed a drink at the Hare & Hounds and of how they had later purchased some whisky and had then gone back to High Ridge Farm with it. There they had drunk a good portion of the whisky before going to bed. Something woke Partington during the early hours, but he claimed he did not recognise the voice and immediately thought he was being robbed. He then lunged at the person in his room and hit him repeatedly with his stump, his crook having earlier been taken out. The pair grappled for a few minutes, before both of them fell down the stairs. He then related how Entwistle did not get up and of how he then discovered that he was dead.

The police thought the pair had got drunk and then quarrelled. A fight broke out and the pair grappled for some time, but repeated blows to the head using the stump of Partington's false arm was what killed Entwistle. They believed Partington intended to kill Entwistle from the start of the fight, because the blows to the head were repeated rather than being just enough force to stop Entwistle from fighting back. A charge of willful murder, it seemed, would only satisfy the police, as it meant the case could go to trial at Manchester Assizes where the death sentence would be sought.

Dr Mitchell's testimony about the thinness of the skull had thrown some doubt on the charge of willful murder, but even so, the fact that repeated blows had been used during the struggle did not bode well for the accused. However, Mitchell hadn't yet finished. There was a chance that further testimony would swing the evidence in Partington's favour.

The Ridge area behind the Hare & Hounds. I was unable to locate the farms, because, I suspect, names have been changed since that time.

Dr Mitchell told those gathered at the inquest that some of the wounds to the head of the deceased were definitely sustained from the stump of Partington's false right arm, but he then complicated matters by stating that the other wounds to the head could easily have been caused by falling downstairs. Mr Butcher then asked a question that was pivotal to the case: 'Could the fall downstairs have killed Thomas Entwistle?' The doctor thought for only a few seconds before giving his answer: 'Yes, the fall downstairs could easily have resulted in the death of Thomas Entwistle.'

What a relief those words must have been to James Partington, who had looked drawn and uncomfortable throughout the proceedings. But what a blow those words must have been to the police, who were seeking that by now elusive verdict of willful murder. The district coroner then sent the jury out to deliberate and they were back only 15 minutes later, having reached their verdict. There was silence throughout the room of the Royal Hotel as the verdict was read.

The jury decided that James Partington, probably as a result of the drink he had partaken of during the previous evening, had woken and mistakenly thought that Thomas Entwistle was robbing him. He had then acted to protect himself and his property, but had not intended to kill Entwistle. It could not be ascertained exactly what did kill the deceased, either the blows from the stump of the accused or the fall down those stairs at High Ridge Farm, so the only possible verdict they could return was one of 'death by misadventure'. Partington left that hearing greatly relieved, but the police were frustrated at the lack of evidence to gain a conviction, though they remained convinced that Partington had murdered his visitor. Unfortunately, only Partington would ever know for sure.

Additional Notes:

James Partington was remanded in custody for a few weeks after the inquest, until he appeared before magistrates where the decision of the jury was heard. Partington was given the chance to speak for himself and he stated that he had woken up that night to discover someone leaning over him. He mistakenly thought the man was a robber and so tackled him. Both men then fell down the stairs and Thomas Entwistle was killed in the fall. Partington said he had been full of remorse ever since.

This was a strange case, as Partington had earlier stated that he heard a voice he did not recognise on waking that night, saying nothing about a man leaning over his bed. On being questioned by the police the day after the incident took place, Partington did not seem in the least remorseful, claiming that he was justified in attacking Entwistle. Certain facts just did not add up, yet the authorities failed to notice these inconsistencies. The magistrates deliberated and decided to uphold the verdict of the inquest. The case against James Partington was dismissed.

CASE SIX   1900

A CALLOUS MURDER THAT SHOCKED THE NATION

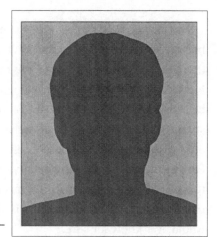

Suspect:	Joseph Holden
Age:	57
Charge:	Murder

Our first crime begins with 9-year-old George Eldred returning home to his mother at No. 48 Ingham Street in Bury. He had been on a day out with his grandfather and was in rather a poor state, with the back of his head cut open and bleeding quite badly. What the boy went on to say was truly shocking to his parents. It was so shocking, in fact, that they just couldn't bring themselves to believe him, which would prove to be a fatal mistake. Perhaps the boy was known as a bit of a liar or perhaps what they were hearing was just so horrifying that the possibility of it being true could not even be contemplated.

'My granddad tried to kill me,' claimed the lad.

The 21 August 1900 had been a glorious day and Joseph Holden took his grandson for a walk in the surrounding countryside, as any normal grandfather would on such a day. They eventually took their rest in a small field at Birtle, around where the old quarry and the Church Inn are situated. It was while resting here that, according to the boy, his grandfather asked him to cut some tobacco. While he carried out this task his grandfather took hold of a stone, probably of the smaller type used for drystone walling or a stray stone from the old quarry nearby, and threw it at him. It hit him hard on the back of his head, cutting it open.

The fields where the attempted murder likely took place.

The injuries to the boy's head would surely have given some credence to his horrific statement, but still his cries went unheeded. His grandfather, 57-year-old Joseph Holden, told a convincing story of how the lad had just gotten in the way of a stone he was throwing. His daughter, Annie Eldred, believed every word.

Joseph Holden was an iron-burner who had worked at a number of the iron foundries in the town of Bury, but work in this industry was unreliable and so at such times he also found employment as a general labourer. Again though, jobs in this line were rather volatile; one week he could be in work and the next he was out of it. There were many unemployed folk in industrial towns in those days and so it wasn't long before Holden found himself out of work once more, but this time alternative employment wasn't forthcoming. In the end it was deemed necessary for him to enter the Bury Workhouse situated at Jericho; a small settlement then, built at the foot of the moors which make up part of the South Pennines. Holden was forced to spend much of the year of 1900 there and it seems he was still living at the workhouse on 21 August.

Life was hard in the workhouse and Holden found it difficult to cope with the harsh conditions and often unsympathetic treatment he received. In the end his other daughter and her husband agreed to let him live with them, at their home in Nuttall Street, Bury, until he could get on his feet again, despite the alleged attack on his grandson. This was a decision the married couple would come to deeply regret within just a few days of Holden moving in with the family.

It became apparent almost immediately that Holden had a problem with drink and this, more than fluctuating market conditions, may have explained why he found it so hard to find and keep employment. Mill towns in those days were full of men who worked hard but also played hard, and heavy drinking and gambling made up a large part of the social activities of the working masses. At that time, miners and quarrymen were common around Bury too and some of these had fearsome reputations. Some of these miners, in fact, would bet on anything with even a slight hint of competition about it. The towns around Manchester were especially prominent with drinking, gambling, whippet racing and rabbit coursing with both whippets and leggy terriers.

Nuttall Street today.

The Manchester terrier had been bred in such districts for rabbit coursing contests, and gambling on these best-of-three competitions was rife, with winners often taking away quite large sums of money. There was also hound trailing (more associated with the Lake District these days, but also common in Pennine areas at the turn of the twentieth century), dog fighting, cock fighting and rat pits, all providing opportunities of losing money faster than it could be printed.

It seems that Joseph Holden had become caught up in such a lifestyle outside of working hours, but life in the workhouse meant he had neither the funds nor the time to spend in such wasteful activities. Many inmates (the common term for those who were compelled to enter such places, which makes the workhouse sound like a prison) were there because they drank and gambled their wages away. Joseph Holden's drinking became problematic very quickly and major rows began to occur between him and his daughter. In the end, out of desperation and wishing to restore peace, his daughter asked him to leave and find alternative accommodation. Reading between the lines of newspaper reports of the account, it seems that by Wednesday, 5 September 1900, Holden had been removed from the family home because of his anti-social behavior. What was going through his mind will never be known, though it now seems obvious that he had been plotting some way of getting back at his daughter for what he may have perceived as a great injustice after he had been put out onto the streets. However, this does not explain why he attacked his 9-year-old grandson back in August, when he was still residing in the workhouse.

Taking an educated guess, I would say that Holden had been living with his daughter Annie at Ingham Street before entering the workhouse at Jericho. She probably evicted him from her home for his exploits with drink, thus forcing him to enter a much harsher life as an inmate of the workhouse, where his drinking and socialising was severely restricted. The guardians of such establishments did not allow alcohol on the premises, unless it was for a special occasion such as at Christmas time, but even then drink was only served if the majority of the guardians voted in favour of allowing it. Very often the Temperance League got involved in the voting and lobbied the guardians until they had a majority against allowing even a glass of ale with Christmas dinner. Holden no doubt resented such strict rules and bitterly blamed his daughters for his lot in life.

Attacking his grandson in the field that day may well have been motivated by a vengeful attitude towards Annie. His other daughter may well have allowed him into her home at the end of August or the beginning of September, in the hopes that his more sober time in the Bury Workhouse had changed him for the better. Tragically, she was wrong.

What's left of Ingham Street.

Meanwhile, George, the 9-year-old son of the Ingham Street couple, was seriously ill due to his injuries as blood poisoning and erysipelas had set in. He was admitted to Bury Infirmary for medical treatment, with his condition so critical that doctors did not know if he would pull through. In the meantime Joseph Holden plotted his schemes and these eventually took him to St Thomas's School where his other grandson, John Dawes, aged only 8, was in attendance. Holden asked to see the schoolmaster and then claimed that the boy's mother wanted him to go on an errand to the Sundial Inn for her, which was of a very important nature, and so could his grandson be excused from school in order to carry out his mother's wishes. The schoolmaster asked Holden why *he* could not carry out the errand for the boy's mother himself, but Holden countered he had to go to Heywood on other business and so could not spare the time. Reluctantly, the schoolmaster agreed to allow John to go, a decision he would regret for the rest of his life. He did state, however, that the boy seemed very content when he went with his grandfather, which suggests there were no problems between them before this time.

Of course the mother's errand was a farce. John must have thought it a little strange when his grandfather passed the Sundial Inn, leading him into the fields above Walmersley and into the old disused Top o'th' Hill Quarry at Limefield, which remains to this day and continues to be disused. If the lad hadn't already sensed that something was wrong, he soon would, as his grandfather took him to the top of the quarry cliffs, now fully intent on carrying out his evil schemes.

Mrs Dawes was oblivious to all these goings-on, of course. What occurred that terrible day did not become clear until later that night when Joseph Holden walked into the police station at Radcliffe and told the desk sergeant that he thought he had drowned his grandson. The desk sergeant then led Holden into a waiting room and there he was interviewed in what proved to be an increasingly disturbed atmosphere. The police who were present at the interview heard one of the most harrowing and disturbing accounts of their whole careers.

Holden first spoke to Sergeant Thomas, confessing that he thought he had drowned his grandson. At first it wasn't clear exactly what had happened and whether or not this drowning had been of an accidental nature, which was no doubt their first and foremost thought. But a little later, while being interviewed by Sergeants Arrowsmith and Swainbank,

The Wagon & Horses on Walmersley Road, which Holden likely passed as he led his grandson to an awful death.

things became much clearer when Holden asked them to lock him up 'for murder'. Holden then went on to explain the unfolding events of that awful day and of how he had led his 8-year-old grandson to certain death. Sergeants Arrowsmith and Swainbank must have been deeply shocked by what they heard that night, despite some of the ghastly things they had already heard and witnessed during their time in the police force.

An old photo of tramlines being laid on Walmersley Road about the time of the murder.

Sergeant Arrowsmith would later disclose what was said in that waiting room to a packed courtroom at the Manchester Assizes. Holden told him that he had led his grandson up onto the quarry cliffs at Limefield and then thrown him down the cliff face, but the boy had landed on some 'soft stuff' (a shaley type of soil still found in profusion at the scene of the crime). Holden then went down to his grandson and took him back up to the cliff tops, now grabbing the boy by the scruff of the neck and the back of his breeches, before hurling him over the edge once more. This time the young boy was more seriously injured and the confessing grandfather (it seems wrong to use such a paternal word) described how the back of his head was badly cut and bleeding. Unbelievably, Holden then went on to tell Sergeant Arrowsmith of how he had picked the boy up once more and took him back up to the top of the cliffs, before hurling him over the edge and into the water below. Then he walked away, leaving the poor boy to his own devices. He said that he did not know the outcome and that would explain why Holden first exclaimed that he *thought* he had drowned his grandson.

Arrowsmith and Swainbank locked up the prisoner for the night and quickly set about organising a search of Limefield Quarry, mustering as many officers as they could for the necessary and unpleasant work ahead. Despite a thorough search through the night, it wasn't until the following morning that the body of the young boy was at last discovered, after Sergeant Swainbank dragged the water of the quarry lodge. (It was known locally as 'the Delph' when I was a boy – a place where many local children played, oblivious of the horrors that had happened decades before.) The battered and bruised body of young John Dawes was found approximately 6ft from the bank, in 6ft of water.

The cliffs where poor John Dawes was thrown from.

He was pulled out shortly and Sergeant Swainbank described to the intently listening courtroom of how the boy was obviously dead but still bleeding profusely from his nose and mouth, as well as from wounds to his head. Particularly bad was a cut on the left side of his forehead and he also had a cut on the side of his left eye. A large cut was found on the back of his head too, which had been sustained during his second fall from the cliff top, according to the prisoner's gruesome account. The sergeant also searched among the nearby rocks and found several bloody marks down the quarry cliffs where the boy had obviously made contact

The 'soft stuff' where John Dawes landed.

as he fell. This was a horrible experience for the officers involved, but must have been agonising for his parents who waited anxiously for information on the whereabouts of their beloved son. They were given the terrible news that morning and may have sorely regretted not believing their nephew

George. Joseph Holden appeared at the Bury Borough Police Court on that same day, charged with the willful murder of John Dawes, his own

'bleeding profusely from his nose and mouth'

grandson, on Thursday, 6 September 1900. He was remanded in custody and committed for trial at the Manchester Assizes.

All of the evidence was presented and heard at the Manchester Assizes on Tuesday, 13 November 1900 where Superintendent Noblett explained the case for the bench. He also explained that Holden had been in the Bury Workhouse and that he had only just come out about a week ago. It was then the turn of Sergeants Thomas, Arrowsmith and Swainbank to give their grisly statements to a shocked courtroom. In fact, this callous murder shocked the whole of the nation as newspaper report after newspaper report was published in towns and cities throughout the country. The early reports of some of these newspapers only touched on what had occurred, stating that they were hearing reports of a child murder in Bury, as though preparing people for the horrendous facts that would very soon appear in print. The trial at the Manchester Assizes attracted huge amounts of publicity and reporters from around the nation gathered in order to compile their stories – stories which, unfortunately, were absolutely true. One of the reports concerned a statement by witness Martha Spencer, who said that she saw Holden and his grandson walking along the road in the direction of Limefield Quarry on the day of the murder.

In the end it did not take long to settle the matter, in spite of the defense claiming that Holden wasn't fit to stand trial on account of insanity, as this was dismissed by experts. Medical experts also testified that John Dawes was still

The water where the little lad was left to drown.

alive when he was thrown into the water, as the cause of death was by drowning. They also said his injuries were sustained just before death and he was fully clothed at the time of drowning, except for a cap and one clog, which were later found at the quarry after Holden told the police they came off as the boy fell. Mrs Dawes, the boy's mother, gave evidence at the trial and it was reported that she wept bitterly whilst doing so. Joseph Holden pleaded guilty to the charges and so sentence was quickly passed, once the evidence had been heard. Justice Darling heard the case and he enforced the only possible punishment he could in those days; Joseph Holden was sentenced to death by hanging. He was to be held at Strangeways Prison until the day of execution, which was set for 4 December 1900.

Holden walked his grandson up this lane leading into the quarry knowing full well what he was going to do to him.

The day of execution finally dawned and Holden, without any hope of reprieve, rose at 6.30 a.m. as was his usual custom, though his night had been a troubled one. During the previous day, Holden had been allowed an interview with his son Wilfred and daughter Annie, with his other daughter now grieving for her dead

It was likely a stone from a drystone wall that Holden used in his attempt to kill George Eldred.

son and understandably staying away. It did not go well and the meeting was reported as a 'painful one', as one can imagine. Young George Eldred, who was recovering from his ordeal by this time, was also present at the prison, but it was deemed expedient to keep him away from his grandfather.

That 'painful' meeting with his son and daughter, as well as the young boy's presence at the prison, may have contributed to the troubled night experienced by the prisoner, adding to the dread and fear he felt as the day of execution approached. He ate only a light breakfast before visitors were due at his cell.

At 7 a.m. the Reverend C. Williams visited the prisoner and he later stated to the press that Holden had been full of remorse and penitence, though one cannot help but wonder why this had not afflicted his conscience after his attempt to murder George Eldred in the field at Birtle, or at least after he had first thrown his other grandson from the quarry cliffs, when his life could easily have been saved after he had landed on that 'soft stuff'?

It is difficult to believe that Holden was truly penitent, as reports state he was 'unconcerned' when attending his trial. At an inquest held in mid-September he was also totally unrepentant, not to mention callous in his attitude toward his grieving daughter who suffered from severe nervous-exhaustion at the inquest when she gave evidence. When Joseph Holden was asked if he had listened to what she had said, he stated that if *she* had been present that day, 'she'd a' had to gone a' down instead o' t' child'. This caused Mrs Dawes a great deal of distress, so I doubt she would have been too impressed by reports of his deep sorrow and penitence on the morning of his execution.

After spending quite a bit of time with the prison chaplain, the executioner, Mr Billington of Bolton, arrived at the condemned man's cell, along with his assistant. Joseph Holden was pinioned in silence and led away to the scaffold for execution. Billington later told reporters that Holden was completely silent throughout the long walk from his cell to the place of execution, but that he had taken a few moments to compose himself before leaving his cell.

A number of people were present for the execution, including Mr C. Williams, Mr Costeker the undersheriff, Mr Edwards and Mr Smith, who were surgeons at Strangeways Prison, Mr R.A. Armitage, the visiting member of the Committee of Justices, the deputy governor, Mr Platt and the prison governor, Mr R.D. Cruikshank. Holden was led onto the scaffold in complete silence. The noose was placed around his neck by Mr Billington, who obviously knew his job well, as reports state that Holden died the moment he dropped and the rope tightened. A few days later questions would be asked in the House of Commons by Mr Ritchie of the Home Office as to whether enough had been done to inquire into the sanity of Joseph Holden, but such questions came too late for him and the premeditated nature of the attempted murder of one grandson, and the actual murder of the other, meant that no other outcome to the case was possible.

Between 300–400 people gathered outside Strangeways Gaol and watched as the black flag signaling Holden's death was hoisted to the top of the flagpole. An inquest into the case and the hanging of the now infamous Joseph Holden, reported to be just a formality, was held later on the day of execution before the county coroner, Mr J.F. Price. The throngs gathered at the prison gates watched silently for several moments as the ominous black flag fluttered in the cold breeze, before they finally began to disperse and drift away, certain that justice had now been carried out for poor little John Dawes.

Additional Notes:

The funeral of young John Dawes, said to be a happy, bright and intelligent child who was popular at school, took place on Monday, 10 September 1900 and even this sad event proved to be full of drama. George Eldred was able to see the funeral procession for a short duration as it made its way to the cemetery in Bury, from his bedroom window, where he was still recovering after being on the brink of death only a few days earlier. It was reported that he wasn't out of danger yet, but thankfully he did go on to make a full recovery.

Just as the funeral procession rounded the corner of the cemetery grounds, a greengrocer's cart went crashing into the first carriage occupied by Mrs Dawes, the grieving mother, and other relatives. One shaft of the cart went through an open window, splintering the sides, while the horse was dashed against the wheel, almost overturning the carriage. No one was injured, but Mrs Dawes was deeply distressed and fainted as a result. A large crowd witnessed this freak accident. The folk of the town of Bury displayed great sympathy to the grieving parents and the rest of the family of John Dawes.

SOLVED

THE BURY LAMP TRAGEDY

Suspect:	Samuel Thompson
Age:	25
Charge:	Murder

An inquest was held on Tuesday, 9 October 1900 into the death of Mrs Annie Thompson, whom, it was alleged, had been willfully murdered by her own husband, Samuel Thompson. Samuel was found guilty of the charge of willful murder by the jury at the inquest, but with a recommendation that the judge show mercy to the prisoner, and was thus committed for trial to Manchester Assizes by magistrates of the Bury Police Court. This took place a few days after the inquest had been concluded, on Wednesday, 17 October 1900. The magistrates at the Bury Police Court upheld the jury's verdict and so a date was set for the trial, which would be held on Tuesday, 13 November 1900 – the same day that Joseph Holden would appear for the vicious murder of his grandson – a fact that would be widely reported by the national media.

Samuel Thompson, aged 25 years at the time of the trial, was a rag-gatherer by trade (known as a 'rag 'n' bone man' in the north) and he lived with his wife at No. 54 Union Square, which no longer exists, this area now being one of stores and car parks which are located close to Bury Town Centre. He was charged with the willful murder of his wife and he gave his defense before the judge, Justice Darling, who also presided over the Holden case. The details that would be heard that day were not pleasant to say the least, as Annie Thompson had died in rather horrific circumstances.

Samuel had allegedly thrown a lighted paraffin lamp at his wife, which had hit her in the face and then set her clothes on fire. She was badly burned, as one can imagine, and was taken to Bury Infirmary for treatment where she sadly died two days later. It needed to be settled whether or not Samuel Thompson had committed such a terrible act with murderous intentions. He, of course, stated that it was not a murderous act but was instead an accident caused by losing his temper after being tormented all day by his wife.

'hit her in the face and then set her clothes on fire'

Samuel Thompson stated before the packed assizes that his wife had been drunk on the day of the tragic incident, which occurred on Saturday, 6 October 1900, and that they had been quarrelling for much of that day, because of her drinking. She returned home from a local inn (there were several in the Union Square district) and asked her husband for more money, but he refused to give it to her. He did go to the nearby King's Head with her, where she began calling him names, possibly because he continued to refuse to give her money and wouldn't buy her a drink either.

She somehow procured more money, though the means of which Samuel failed to disclose (no doubt he weakened and gave her more money in the end), as he later took money off her and told her to go to bed. All of this took place in the afternoon and Annie must have sobered up by that evening, as she and her husband made up. But, according to Samuel Thompson, she then got drunk again and began dancing around the house, so they quarrelled once more. She then told him that a chap named Crowe was a better man than he, mocking and tormenting him, at which he then lost his temper and knocked the lamp out of her hand and it went all over her.

Penitence struck Samuel immediately, however, as the gravity of what he had done hit home. He tried to put out the flames and his hands were quite badly burned in the process. He explained how, afterwards, once his wife had been attended to by the doctor, taken away to Bury Infirmary and suffered terrible pain until she died two days later, he wandered the streets of Bury 'not in my right mind'.

Expert testimony was called on at the trial and Dr Bailey said that death had been caused 'by spasms of glottis caused by burns', which did not really surprise anyone, though it had to be confirmed by an expert because of legal requirements. Mary Stott, Annie Thompson's aunt, described to the court how, on Saturday night at 10.45 p.m., her niece had run into her house with her stays and breast covered in sparks and her dress saturated with paraffin. She then cried out to her aunt, 'Oh, send for a doctor.' Annie was in terrible pain and distress, but it seems that the flames had been extinguished before she ran round to Mary Stott's house. Mary Stott then went on to say that 'it was obvious she had been drinking' which backed up the testimony given by Samuel Thompson that his wife had been drunk that day. Although she ran to her aunt for help, Mary Stott's niece did not tell her what had happened for her to be burnt in such a terrible manner.

Annie Thompson was able to speak to the police before she died and she stated that she and her husband had argued over a little girl staying with them. He did not want her to stay, while his wife did. She said they quarrelled and he then lost his temper and threw the lamp at her, which hit her on the mouth, spilling paraffin all over her which then set alight, being ignited by the wick of the lamp. It turned out in court that a little girl was indeed at the house and her testimony would shed much doubt on the truthfulness of what Thompson was telling the police and the court.

Nellie Scott was just 8 years of age when she gave evidence in court and she told the packed hearing that during an argument with Annie Thompson, Samuel Thompson lost his temper and threw the lamp at his wife while standing close to her. She said that he picked the lamp up from off the table before throwing it, but that she did not see where it struck Annie, as by this time she was frightened and ran upstairs. This was important testimony, when used in conjunction with Constable Mathieson's evidence and description of the events surrounding the charging of Samuel Thompson with the willful murder of his wife.

On being charged, Samuel had said to Constable Mathieson that he did not throw the lamp at all, but that 'she [meaning his wife, Annie] picked it up and I knocked it out of her hand'. Samuel Thompson then told Constable Mathieson that her death had been caused 'through aggravation'. His version of events then, was different to that of both Annie Thompson and the little girl, Nellie Scott, who witnessed the scene. The court, and more importantly the jury, could now not believe anything Samuel said. He had been exposed as a liar, though his badly burned hands confirmed his testimony that he had immediately made efforts to put out the flames.

After all of the testimony had been heard and the witnesses had appeared before judge and jury, the prisoner was asked if he had anything to say regarding what had been discussed during the hearing. He simply said, 'I did not intend doing the thing I did, but she had tormented me all afternoon, and at night. In aggravation I didn't know what I was doing.' The jury retired to consider their verdict.

After a period of time the jury returned and they found Samuel Thompson not guilty of willful murder, but guilty of manslaughter. Justice Darling passed sentence after the verdict had been read and Thompson was to serve ten years in penal servitude for his crime.

Additional Notes:

The outcome could have been quite different for Samuel Thompson, as his lies had done him no favours. The testimony of Annie Thompson just before she died was harmonious with that of little Nellie Scott and such testimony could easily have condemned the prisoner to a death sentence, but peculiar to those times was sympathy for a man who quarrelled with his wife. The wife was always portrayed as the tormentor, the nagger, the belligerent of the pair and it is amazing how many cases of this, and earlier periods, were influenced by the man getting the sympathy of judge and jury simply because the husband felt tormented and goaded by his 'argumentative wife'.

A CRUEL AND ATROCIOUS MURDER

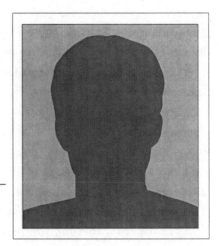

Suspect:	William Goacher
Age:	?
Charge:	Murder

William Goacher was a millwright at one of the many mills situated in Bury and he was described by friends as an 'innocent and inoffensive man'. But his life was about to take an unexpected turn that changed many people's opinion of a man who was once their friend. The evening of 5 March 1901 saw William Goacher drinking at the Cricketer's Arms which was situated between Union Square and the Mosses area of Bury, approximately 5 minutes' walk from his terraced home at Spring Street. This public house no longer exists, but the terraced brick houses of Spring Street remain. Mr Goacher enjoyed his drink and he seems to have been out most nights of the week, but those who knew him stated that they had never known him to be drunk. This suggests he was a modest drinker, if these witnesses are to be believed.

His wife had become increasingly disturbed by his gallivanting, however, as he often stayed out until midnight or even 1 a.m. on occasion. He was out in the early hours on the night of 5/6 March and it seems that 57-year-old Mrs Goacher had by this time had enough, as she locked him out of the house and wouldn't answer his knocks and pleas to be let in. It seems the Cricketer's Arms was a sure place for a bit of 'after hours' drinking, but the place was closed when he returned there, possibly seeking a bed for the night. The other inns were also closed and it wasn't until 6.30 a.m. that he was able to rouse William Holden, a friend of his who was the landlord of the nearby Commercial Hotel. Holden gave Goacher a warming whisky and gin before he left, hoping his wife was by this time up and about and willing to let him into their home.

Mrs Goacher did let him into their home, but events then took a decided turn for the worse. Soon neighbours heard a terrified voice cry 'murder' and 'help'. What happened became clearer at an inquest held on 1 April 1901 after a number of witnesses, mostly close neighbours of the Goachers, gave evidence to a packed hearing, though some confusion as to the actual truth of those events still remained. Two versions of what happened were presented before the inquest into Mrs Goacher's death on 29 March 1901, but a later trial at Manchester Assizes would settle once and for all which version was accurate.

The first witness to appear before the inquest on 1 April was Agnes Calderbank of Spring Street, who stated quite emphatically that Mr and Mrs Goacher were 'always quarrelling'. On 6 March, Calderbank heard the aforementioned cries of 'murder' and 'help,' which resulted in her going round to the house at Spring Street and knocking furiously on the door. William Goacher answered her knock rather reluctantly and what she saw in the interior of the living room rather shocked her, to say the least. Mrs Goacher was lying on the sofa in a very poor state of health, having been badly burned on her head, face and arms. Mrs Goacher then said, 'I haven't done it, he's done it.'

'I haven't done it, he's done it.'

Agnes Calderbank told William Goacher to go and fetch a doctor, but Mrs Goacher said, 'Tha murdering thing, tha doesn't want a doctor, it's th'alehouse tha wants.' She then told Calderbank that her husband had held her to the living room fire with his shoes over his hands, but then Goacher stepped in and stopped her from saying any more. However, she would not be silenced and went on to say, 'You know you have done it,' while looking at her husband. Goacher became very agitated and replied, 'No, no, don't tell that to anyone again,' but she repeated that he had done it to her and that it was no accident, but added that she 'didn't want any bother'. Mrs Goacher died of these appalling burns in Bury Infirmary on 29 March.

William Goacher was present at the inquest to hear all of this evidence, being represented by Mr Birtwistle, but he did not seem unduly worried. He protested his innocence while being guarded by two police officers (he had been held in custody since the death of his wife a few days earlier). He wasn't concerned because Mrs Goacher, once the doctor arrived, told him that her husband hadn't done anything to her and she had fallen against the oven. Also, Mr Bull, Borough Magistrates Clerk, produced Mrs Goacher's depositions taken just before her death when she stated that she had indeed quarrelled with her husband on 6 March, but that he hadn't caused her injuries, repeating once again that she had fallen against the oven.

This threw the proverbial spanner into the works, despite the doctor giving evidence that the injuries were not consistent with falling against an oven but were likely received after being very close to an open fire for a considerable length of time. Seeds of doubt had been sown and so the inquest concluded with an 'open verdict'. Goacher would appear before the bench three times and on his third appearance he was committed for trial at Manchester Assizes, to be held on Monday, 22 April 1901 at the Crown Court.

The trial was heard before Justice Wills, with Mr Sutton and Mr A.H. Maxwell prosecuting. Defending the accused was Mr Roe-Rycroft. The prisoner was present throughout, looking very pale and far older than his actual age. It was also reported that Mr Goacher's demeanor before the court gave the impression that he had not quite grasped the seriousness of the charges against him. Mr Goacher then heard the charges and pleaded 'not guilty' before a packed courtroom, hopeful of being found not guilty because of his wife telling the police and the doctor that she had fallen against the oven, and evidence was to come out that would in some small way support her claim. Julia Langton confirmed that Mr and Mrs Goacher were always quarrelling and she also said that Mrs Goacher had been bad on her legs for a number of years so was often falling, but her injuries were so severe that it was deemed by a number of expert witnesses that these were not consistent with falling against an oven. Agnes Calderbank gave her evidence again, as she had done at the inquest. Then more witnesses were called.

Julia Langton also lived in Spring Street. She stated that she often heard the married couple next door arguing and although Goacher regularly came home very late, she had never seen him drunk. This suggests that William Goacher was no more than a social drinker, that is, one who went to local public houses more for the company than for the drink. As a millwright, which involved highly skilled work (*See* Additional Notes), Goacher would have earned good money and so could no doubt have afforded to get drunk most nights of the week if he was that way inclined. Langton's statement supported his sobriety.

Spring Street today. The row of houses where the Goacher's lived was demolished years ago.

It was also stated that on 6 March, Mrs Langton heard screams of 'murder' and 'help', so she went to the front door and attempted to let herself in, but the door was locked. She knocked furiously, but no one answered, so she went round to the back door but this too was locked. She then began kicking the back door and Goacher eventually answered. Mrs Langton then saw Mrs Goacher lying on the floor in a very bad state, with severe burns to her face, arms and hands. Mrs Goacher told her neighbour that Mr Goacher had knelt on her and that he 'tried to murder me'. Mrs Langton then called Goacher a 'scoundrel' and in response he ordered her out of the house.

It seems that Mrs Langton was the first on the scene. Agnes Calderbank and the others who eventually went to investigate did not act immediately when they heard the cries for help, as the Goachers were always arguing and their neighbours were used to hearing it. When Detective John Porter arrived at the scene Mrs Goacher told him that her husband had done it to her, but that she didn't want any bother. Goacher then told Porter that he had been out drinking at the Cricketer's Arms and when he had returned home she was already badly burned. Goacher had earlier gone round to the local shop owned by a Mr Brady and had told the proprietor that his wife had been drinking and had fallen onto the fire. Annie Brady, the daughter of the shopkeeper, would also give evidence to the court and she said that she heard Mrs Goacher screaming, 'He's murdering me, fetch the police.' It seems she did not act as, again, Annie Brady had often heard them quarrelling, so Mrs Goacher's cries were not taken seriously.

A doctor had been sent for after Detective Porter attended the scene and this was Dr Braithwaite, who ordered Mrs Goacher's removal to Bury Infirmary as her condition was very serious. Dr Braithwaite was one of the expert witnesses who stated that the burns to Mrs Goacher's hands, face and arms were just too severe to have occurred through falling against an oven door. He was of the opinion that she must have been lying against the greater heat of the open fire for some considerable time to have received such severe burns. With multiple witnesses having been told it was Mr Goacher, as well as another witness, Rachael Hart, who was also told by Mrs Goacher that her husband had done it to her, the suggestion that she fell against an oven door was very quickly collapsing. Goacher had sternly denied any wrongdoing throughout, but the witness statements were by now building up into a rather damning report. Goacher's confidence would surely have lessened somewhat by this time.

Frederick William Porter, a joiner at Walmersley in Bury, was called before the court and regarded as an expert on the heat of ovens. He stated that an oven could not get hot enough to cause the severe burns that had occurred to parts of Mrs Goacher's body. Dr Molineux, a house surgeon at Bury Infirmary who treated Mrs Goacher's injuries, agreed completely with what Mr Porter had told the court. However, Goacher, his spirits now no doubt very low, was rather heartened by what Dr Mitchell had to say to the court when called by the defense. He was of the expert opinion that Mrs Goacher, because of her bad legs and the possibility of her having been drinking, could have fallen by accident, but that she must have been right next to the open fire for some time and not the oven door. The defense was trying to make out that Mrs Goacher had been drinking, become confused and so fell into the fire.

The defense also called Detective John Porter, who stated that Goacher had vehemently denied harming his wife. On arresting William Goacher the accused said to Detective Porter, 'I am not charged with that [the willful murder of his wife], I didn't do anything.' Rachael Hart also told the court that, after Mrs Goacher had accused her husband of doing her harm, he stated, 'I have not.' Goacher, however, declined to give evidence, either at the inquest or in court.

The case had by this time become a little confusing and the evidence wasn't exactly adding up. One thing which had been firmly established was that the severity of the burns to Mrs Goacher's arms, hands and face could not have been received as a result of her falling against the oven; only the heat of open flames could have caused such injuries. The statements of Mrs Goacher were varied too. First she had said that her husband was responsible for her burns and that he had acted deliberately, with the full intention of murdering her. But then she had claimed it was an accident after all. She was bad on her legs and often fell: that was also established in court. However, even after saying this, she told doctors and Detective Porter that her husband had indeed done it, but that she 'didn't want any bother'. She told her neighbours that he had held her down with shoes over his hands, but then went on to tell others that he had knelt on her, which also caused some confusion and maybe a little doubt, but the prosecution easily explained that one away by stating that he knelt on her and held her with his shoes over his hands. The prosecution also explained some of the irregularities in the statements of the deceased by stating that she would be confused to some extent after going through such a traumatic and excruciatingly painful experience. All such things were deliberated by the jury who had heard the evidence at the Manchester Assizes that day.

Such deliberations only took half an hour to conclude and the jury were soon back in court. The judge asked the appointed representative to stand and pronounce the verdict of the jury and this was a resounding 'we find the prisoner guilty of willful murder'. Goacher's demeanor was now quite different to what it had been earlier in the trial, especially when he heard the judge pass the death sentence, to be carried out at the nearby Strangeways Prison. Before dismissing Goacher from the court, the judge looked him straight in the eye and stated that his was a particularly 'cruel and atrocious murder'.

It seems that Goacher had some very loyal friends and family, as they campaigned for a reprieve, which was granted by the Home Secretary on 11 May 1901, just before he was due to be hanged. The prison governor informed William Goacher as soon as he heard the news and it was reported that the prisoner was greatly relieved. He was allowed to communicate with his family and friends soon after being given the verdict of the Home Office. And what was the reason given by the Home Secretary for such a reprieve? Because it was decided that Goacher's wife had so provoked him to roast her to death that he did not deserve the full penalty of the law!

Additional Notes:

A millwright was a highly skilled craftsman who was involved in the construction of machinery. They were experts in carpentry and built and maintained machines mostly used in the manufacture of lumber, paper, agriculture and food during those early days of industry. However, by the time of William Goacher the skills of millwrights had been increased to include the building and maintenance of machines used in the textile mills of the north, which is the industry Goacher worked in. Goacher would not only have worked with timber, but also with steel and other materials. Many of these millwrights worked as independent contractors, though several were employed at just one mill. If Goacher was an independent contractor, then he would have earned even better money than if he had been in the employment of one of the local mills.

DEATH OF A SWEETHEART

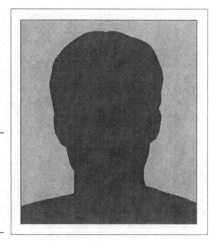

Suspects:	Tom Earnshaw and John Bottomley
Ages:	19 and 45
Charge:	Murder

Tom Earnshaw was just 19 years of age when he met Nellie Stephenson; a 20-year-old millworker who lived with her adoptive, elderly parents in Deal Street, Bury. The pair began courting early in the year of 1903 and by early spring they were seeing a lot of each other and spending much of their spare time together. It is true to say they became sweethearts, but it is not known if they had met each other's parents, or how serious their relationship had become. By early April of 1903, Nellie Stephenson had some news for Earnshaw which he was far from pleased to hear. Stephenson had become pregnant out of wedlock and, because of the times she was living in and that her elderly parents relied on her for income, she wished to have the baby aborted. Earnshaw gave his consent and the arrangements were rather swiftly made. Exactly what happened then was never fully ascertained, but it did result in a trial being held at Liverpool Assizes on Monday, 11 May 1903, where Tom Earnshaw, together with 45-year-old John Bottomley, found himself charged with willful murder.

Justice Lawrance presided over the trial and Mr A.G. Steel, K.C. together with Mr Mansfield, appeared for the prosecution, while Mr Overend Evans stood for the defense. Tom Earnshaw and John Bottomley were both charged with the willful murder of Nellie Stephenson on 21 April 1903 and both pleaded not guilty. An unusual step was then taken by the prosecuting lawyers, Mr Steel and Mr Mansfield, of telling the packed court hearing that the prosecution would not be seeking capital punishment, as they felt that the circumstances resulting in the trial did not warrant such a severe conclusion. Earnshaw was thus

The last remaining old houses on Deal Street today.

acquitted of the capital charge, but was remanded for further, lesser charges to be brought. Bottomley, however, continued to be tried for willful murder and if found guilty there was every chance he would hang.

Nellie Stephenson was a cotton-operative at a mill in Bury and she gave two depositions as she lay dying, which were read in court. These depositions were read out to those in attendance by the Clerk of the Assizes, Sir Herbert Stephens. What she had said before her sad and untimely death was pretty damning evidence, so the defense did their utmost to convince the jury that the testimony of the dying girl could not be relied upon to be absolute truth.

Stephenson said that she had been told about Bottomley by Tom Earnshaw, after she had revealed to him that she was pregnant, but could not keep the baby as her elderly parents relied on her wages coming into the house. Was she hoping that Earnshaw would propose and offer to support her and her elderly parents after she had explained her difficult circumstances to him? It is impossible to say, but it was very unlikely that a 19-year-old shop assistant could have earned enough to keep a family of his own anyway, let alone his in-laws too. If she was hoping for such a positive response from her sweetheart, then she would have been bitterly disappointed, as he told her about John Bottomley and the illegal abortions he carried out for any young girl who went to him in trouble. It became obvious that Earnshaw did not wish to be a responsible father and only wanted the trouble to go away before their parents found out what had been going on.

She thus made an appointment with John Bottomley through Tom Earnshaw and went to see him on 15 April at his herbal shop in Bolton Street, Bury. The premises of which belonged to Bottomley's 75-year-old father who likely did not know of such proceedings being carried out at his home, as he was never implicated in any way, either before or during the trial. Stephenson explained her difficulties to Bottomley and he arranged for her to return on Wednesday, 20 April when he would carry out the illegal abortion. She returned on that date and Bottomley carried out the procedure in a back room of his business premises. She paid Bottomley 10s for the procedure, monies which were provided by Tom Earnshaw.

All seemed well, but the day after the operation, on 21 April 1903, Nellie Stephenson fell seriously ill and her condition rapidly deteriorated. It was thought urgent to take depositions and two were recorded, both of which were read out in court. In the second deposition it was recorded that she had said, 'I am dying and I don't think I shall get better.' She proved no false prophet in this regard, as she sadly passed away that same day. The police were called in and Sergeant Gregson was the arresting officer. He arrested both Bottomley and Earnshaw and while at the herbalist's shop Gregson found medical instruments on the premises, which were later blamed for the death of Nellie Stephenson.

A lane off Bolton Street near to where the shop was located.

Dr Johnson gave evidence in court and explained how he had carried out a thorough examination of the body during a post-mortem and his conclusions were that she had died from septic peritonitis. The prosecution asked him how this infection could have been caused and Dr Johnson was adamant that the improper use of the medical instrument involved was the cause. 'No natural cause could possibly have resulted in such a fatal infection,' he concluded. Dr Mitchell corroborated Dr Johnson's findings and the jury was left in no doubts that the operation, or rather, the instrument used in the operation, was the cause of the infection and subsequent death of Nellie Stephenson.

The defense could not question those findings now, so they concentrated on attempting to pull to pieces the depositions recorded by the victim and to demonstrate reasonable doubt concerning John Bottomley's role in the whole sordid business. In fact, they put the whole of the blame on Nellie herself, even attempting to convince the jury that Nellie had performed the operation on herself and that nobody else was involved in any way.

Testimony was also given by the clerk of the assizes to the effect that John Bottomley was taken into the presence of the dying Nellie Stephenson on 20 April and was accused face to face of carrying out the procedure which had resulted in such tragic consequences. Still Bottomley had denied all knowledge of the circumstances surrounding such charges, stating that she had carried out the operation herself and only herself was to blame. He stuck to this defense in court, with the full support of his lawyer. On reading the depositions, Herbert Stephens explained that Miss Stephenson had clearly identified Bottomley as the man whom she went to see on 15 April and again on 20 April when the operation was carried out. Bottomley again denied that he was involved and maintained such denials throughout.

The defense lawyer told the jury that the instruments found on the premises of the herbalist's shop were common and could be found at any medical establishment, stating that nothing could be further from John Bottomley's mind than to cause anyone harm in any way. The defense then reminded the jury that the deceased had been a willing accomplice in the affair, stating that the jury must decide whether or not Bottomley had any part in the proceedings leading up to her death, as well as that there was no corroborative evidence as Nellie Stephenson was dead. However, the two depositions she had recorded before her death made an impression on the jury and such testimony, admissible in court, could not simply be dismissed, though the defense did their utmost to influence the jury to go in such a direction. Justice Lawrance eventually intervened, after the defense had tried their hardest to discredit the depositions of the victim, by stating that the jury must consider such depositions whilst making a decision. He also asked them to note that John Bottomley, when asked to give his final defense before the court, was unwilling to do so and remained silent.

Bottomley stuck to his story, stating that he had nothing to do with the case and that Nellie Stephenson had carried out the procedure on herself, without his knowledge. The jury retired to consider all of the evidence, but it wasn't long before they returned and their verdict was read out. They found John Bottomley not guilty of willful murder, but guilty of manslaughter. Justice Lawrance deferred passing sentence on Bottomley, until the case against Tom Earnshaw was concluded, which was heard immediately after Bottomley's trial had ended.

Tom Earnshaw's charge of willful murder had been dropped, but he now stood before judge and jury on a charge of supplying Nellie Stephenson with noxious drugs. Mr Gibbons stood for the defense, while Mr Steel and John Mansfield again stood for the prosecution. The two depositions read out earlier in the case against John Bottomley were read once more and letters written to Nellie Stephenson by Tom Earnshaw were also produced. A Mr Parkinson, a friend of Earnshaw, appeared as a witness and he stated that Earnshaw had never mentioned anything to do with an abortion, but that he had simply told him that she was in trouble. He also stated that Earnshaw had sent money to Nellie Stephenson for her to buy medicine for the good of her health, as Earnshaw had been concerned about her welfare.

A number of witnesses appeared for the defense and they gave testimony to Tom Earnshaw being a young man of good character. However, the prosecution had a trump card up their sleeve when they asked the arresting officer to give testimony to the court. The officer stated that Earnshaw, on being arrested, had told him he had given Nellie Stephenson money in order to 'remove the trouble'. An awful way to refer to his baby and no doubt such a statement made an impression on the jury. However, the defense came back with testimony to the effect that

Earnshaw had provided funds in order for her to see a doctor and not for an operation to be carried out for the removal of the baby.

Once again the jury retired to consider the evidence and once again they did not take long to reach a decision. The jury found Tom Earnshaw guilty of supplying Nellie Stephenson with noxious drugs, but they asked the court to show mercy in passing sentence. Now time for the sentence to be passed, John Bottomley and Tom Earnshaw stood side by side in the dock, nervously awaiting their fate. Both looked pale and drawn and they fidgeted as they awaited the judge's pleasure.

Justice Lawrance at last spoke. He stated that, though he had been found not guilty of murder, Bottomley's illegal activities had been known for some years now: an illegal business with a reputation of being open to any young girl who found herself in trouble. The judge sternly told Bottomley that he considered him responsible for a great deal of the immorality in Bury at the time. He then sentenced John Bottomley to fifteen years in penal servitude.

Justice Lawrance then turned his attention to Tom Earnshaw, stating that his youth would be taken into consideration, as well as the recommendation for the court to show mercy. He reminded the young man that he had already spent three weeks in prison, so would pass a sentence of three weeks imprisonment, which he had already served on remand, so was now free to go.

Additional Notes:

On both sentences having been passed, the judge then turned to John Bottomley and asked if he would keep the young Tom Earnshaw in his employment at the herbalist shop. The newspapers did not report Bottomley's reply, but it seems likely that he complied with the court's wishes, if, indeed, he was able to keep his business afloat while serving his long sentence. Headlines were afterwards concerned with what was regarded as a 'Heavy Sentence' by many, with regard to John Bottomley rather than Tom Earnshaw, but it was obvious that Bottomley had carried out the operation that led to the death of Nellie Stephenson, and that he had been carrying out such procedures for a number of years. Sadly, it took somebody to die before his illegal activities were at last put to an end.

THE ATTEMPTED MURDER OF A NEIGHBOUR

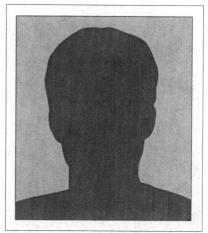

Suspect: John Cuttle

Age: 56

Charge: Murder

Just before noon on Thursday, 2 July 1914 a shot rang out into the air of a quiet terraced street and a resident fell to the floor, blood pouring from a serious wound in his neck. It was the horrific culmination of a peaceful everyday scene that had seen John Grundy quietly trimming the privet hedge which surrounded his small, neatly kept front garden. Fifty-six-year-old John Cuttle who lived at Chester Street, Chesham, had

'blood pouring from a serious wound in his neck'

been responsible for firing the shot, which now attracted attention from a number of folk in the area. The gun was eventually taken from him and the police arrested Cuttle. Justice moved pretty swiftly after that and Cuttle found himself in court that very afternoon, after having been taken to the police office at Bury Town Hall.

Cuttle appeared before the Bury Borough Court and was charged with the attempted murder of John Grundy who was a retired grocer. Grundy was now in the Bury Infirmary being treated by Doctor Holmes, who stated that he would not be capable of attending court in the very near future, if indeed he survived his wounds, which were considered as serious and life threatening. Superintendent Pickering asked that John Cuttle be

A row of houses on Chester Street, where the drama unfolded in 1914.

remanded in custody in order that witnesses and other evidence could be gathered. The court granted the remand and so Cuttle would remain in custody until Grundy, if he lived, could appear in order to give evidence.

A picture of what had occurred that morning began to be pieced together and it seems that John Cuttle had simply walked out of his house with no hat or coat on and had then reached into his pocket and pulled out a pistol, or revolver. John Grundy had been clipping the privet hedge around his front garden and basically minding his own business when Cuttle pulled out the revolver from his pocket and aimed it straight at him. Grundy did not have time to react as Cuttle pulled the trigger and the bullet hit him in the face, knocking him to the ground and spilling blood everywhere.

John Cuttle then threatened others in the area with the revolver, until he was finally persuaded to hand the gun over to his wife. A doctor and the police soon arrived at the scene and Grundy was quickly taken to Bury Infirmary, which was situated just across Clarence Park less than a mile from Chester Street where the incident occurred. The bullet had actually passed through the tongue of John Grundy, knocking a tooth out in the process, before passing through his neck and exiting out the back, when it struck the bricks and front door of Grundy's house. The windpipe of the victim was also found to be slightly injured. Such injuries were obviously serious, but news soon came from Doctor Holmes that Grundy was very likely to recover.

John Cuttle again appeared before the bench on Saturday, 4 July and again Superintendent Pickering asked that proceedings be postponed and Cuttle remanded in custody until the following Saturday, when it was hoped John Grundy would be capable of attending court. The doctors were hopeful that he would be well enough to appear, but they could not be certain. Mr T.R. Bertwistle was representing Cuttle and he had no objections to the case being postponed for another week. And so the court remanded Cuttle in custody and set a date for the following Saturday. However, Grundy was still not well enough to appear in court, so Cuttle was yet again remanded in custody by the bench on Saturday, 11 July, with the next date set for the following Monday.

John Cuttle appeared before the bench once more on Monday, 20 July 1914 and once again Superintendent Pickering was compelled to request yet another remand, as John Grundy, though making good progress, was still too unwell to appear and give evidence. Proceedings could not continue without him, so Cuttle was remanded in custody again until Monday, 27 July, when, finally, Grundy was able to leave hospital in order to attend court and give his crucial evidence.

Although in obvious discomfort and with his recovery having still some way to go, John Grundy managed to give clear evidence to those in attendance; the interest in this case had grown and attracted much media attention. Grundy stated that he and John Cuttle had been neighbours for the past couple of years, but that there had not been any trouble between them, not so much as a slight disagreement. However he did state that, although he had attempted to make conversation with Mr Cuttle on a number of occasions, he had not responded. In fact, he had not uttered as much as one word in reply. Under normal circumstances this would surely have created much tension between neighbours, but Grundy understood that Cuttle had a history of mental illness and that, when Cuttle lived in Hamilton Street, he had been taken away and had spent some time in the Prestwich Mental Asylum, and so Grundy did not allow Cuttle's unfriendly ways to upset him. The portrait painted by John Grundy of the prisoner was one of a quiet and inoffensive man who was obviously troubled in some way.

Alice Bridge now gave evidence. She was related to John Grundy and was also his housekeeper. She said that she was busy with chores in the house when she heard a gunshot outside the front door. She rushed out and found Grundy badly injured, with blood pouring out of his mouth and neck. He was able to get up and

One of the backyards where people hid during the shooting.

she helped him into the house. She said that she saw John Cuttle holding the gun and that he even pointed it at her, but she was able to get into the house and to safety. She had known Cuttle for two or three years and described him in much the same way as Grundy, confirming that he had been confined at Prestwich Lunatic Asylum for some months. She said that the accused never spoke to anyone that she knew of and that he had 'a vacant look'. She also confirmed that there had not been any kind of grievance between them.

Mrs Eliza Duckworth of Chester Street, the wife of Alexander Duckworth, appeared to give evidence and she stated that she had heard a gunshot not long before noon and had gone outside to investigate. John Cuttle then came towards her so she ran into the house and locked her door. Arthur James Ormerod of Bridge Street also heard the gun going off and went into Chester Street, where he saw Cuttle wielding the gun while his wife attempted to persuade him to give it up to her. Cuttle had a go at Ormerod and so he, along with Alexander Robertson of Brierly Street in Bury (in Chester Street carrying out work for the Singer sewing machine company), got into a yard and bolted the door. Afterwards the two men joined Mrs Cuttle in trying to persuade her husband to give up the gun. He finally acquiesced and handed the gun to Mrs Cuttle. Alexander Robertson then took the gun from her and put it away in his pocket, determined that John Cuttle would never again get his hands on it and threaten lives. Ormerod also confirmed that Cuttle had been suffering mental problems for a number of years and had spent time in Prestwich Lunatic Asylum.

Doctor Holmes of Bury Infirmary had attended the scene shortly after the shooting and he described the terrible injuries which could so easily have been fatal. He told of how the bullet had passed through the mouth, knocking a tooth out, and of how it had exited at the back of Grundy's neck. He then noticed the marks on the brickwork and door where the bullet had struck, and found the offending article just 4 yards from the front door. All the evidence now having been heard, Cuttle was committed to the Manchester Assizes for trial.

John Cuttle appeared before Justice Darling at the Manchester Assizes on Tuesday, 17 November 1914 and pleaded not guilty to the charge of shooting with intent to murder. Mr Jackson stood for the defense, while Mr Roe Rycroft stood for the prosecution. The defense brought out in court that Cuttle had a distinguished military career serving in the East Lancashire Regiment where he fought in the Afghan campaign under Lord Roberts. He had also served in the Ashanti and South Africa wars. He had retired about eleven years ago after being invalided home to Plymouth, where he was confined to his bed for seven long years. Whilst serving in the army abroad in a number of campaigns, Cuttle had suffered from malaria several times and once from sunstroke, which made it impossible for him to continue in the Armed Forces. These illnesses had also affected his mind, as he had suffered from delusions and occasionally hallucinations since then. His pension amounted to approximately 9s per day.

Doctor East, the prison medic, was of the opinion that Cuttle was not of sound mind and it was brought out that the prisoner often thought that people were after him in order to put electric shocks into him, which may have been due to the treatment he had received at Prestwich Lunatic Asylum. What became clear was that John Cuttle did indeed suffer from serious mental illness. The jury agreed. After a short deliberation the jury found that Cuttle was insane and an order for detention as a criminal lunatic during His Majesty's pleasure was made. It is unlikely that the prisoner was ever set free.

Additional Notes:

John Cuttle, despite his ill state of mind and lengthy confinement which would undoubtedly have lasted for the rest of his life, still had a wife to support and so during the conclusion of the trial Jackson brought out that he was fearful that Cuttle's pension would be stopped and that his wife would be left destitute. Jackson was diligent in his defense of the prisoner, as he then went on to relate, not only the fine service record of John Cuttle himself, but also that of his family.

The lawyer for the defense brought it to the court's attention that Cuttle's grandfather had fought in the Peninsular War and at Waterloo, having a fine record of service in such campaigns. His father had also been a military man, serving in the Rifle Brigade. He also reminded the court of Cuttle's own record of twenty-nine years in military service. Two of his sons served abroad in the forces too, with one seeing action in South Africa during the Boer War. He was wounded at Marne and sent home. His other son served in France. His wife's grandfather fought in the Crimean War and her grandmother was a nurse who served alongside Florence Nightingale. Her father served as a drummer for twenty-one years in the 73rd Regiment and was now serving in Black Watch. Justice Darling took all such things into consideration and stated that John Cuttle's pension was safe, due to his military service record and the fact that Cuttle could not be held responsible for his actions due to his state of mind, which had been caused by illnesses contracted whilst serving in the military.

FOUR CASES OF MURDER AND SUICIDE

The Case of a Millworker's Wife

It was an idyllic little village and Samuel Kay and his wife Sarah lived in a row of five cottages at Hollyhurst, situated between Whitefield and Radcliffe which were boroughs of Bury. Sarah had once been the wife of a man named Smith, who was a Mormon by faith. He had gone to Salt Lake City and died, leaving his wife with their 5-year-old daughter, Mary Alice Smith. After the death of her husband, Sarah Smith had married Samuel Kay who worked as a power-loom tackler at a mill situated just 5 minutes' walk from their home at Hollyhurst Village. Sarah also worked at the mill, which was owned by a Mr Buckley. Young Mary Alice Smith attended a local village school while her mother and stepfather were working at the mill. By the spring of 1859 Samuel and Sarah Kay were having marital difficulties that would shortly end in tragedy.

One Sunday at the beginning of May, Samuel Kay went out for the day, leaving his wife and stepdaughter at home. He did not return home until 10 p.m., which made Sarah more than a little unhappy. She was then told by an unspecified person that her husband had been seen in improper company with his cousin, which caused the couple to quarrel. They argued on and off for the next three weeks, with Samuel Kay denying that he had been in company with any other woman in an improper way, and Sarah finding it difficult to believe him. She was later described as a sensitive person and as a result was greatly disturbed by the gossip she had heard regarding her husband. He tried over and over again to reassure her, but the quarrel continued to flare up time and again, the accusations made against her husband continually preying on her mind.

On Monday, 23 May 1859, Sarah again raised the by now very sensitive subject of her husband's Sunday outing and this caused yet another quarrel to break out between them. They went to work at the mill and at dinner time came out of the mill together, heading back to their nearby cottage for their meal. On leaving the mill a woman complained to Sarah because she had been speaking disrespectfully of her cousin. This person, I assume, was the one whom Samuel Kay was supposedly in improper company with during that Sunday of three weeks before. This caused her and Samuel to quarrel even more and dinner time was even more strained. Mrs Butterworth, a neighbour, heard them quarrelling and at one point heard Samuel say, 'Get thy dinner and go to thy work.' Samuel heated his dinner in the oven and then put it back in to keep warm for his wife and stepdaughter. He then returned to the mill alone, expecting his wife to be along shortly. What happened then resulted in an inquest being heard before the county coroner, Mr S. Rutter, at the Bay Horse Inn, Chapelfield, just two days later on 25 May 1859. The evidence would shock the town, as well as the nation.

Samuel Kay gave evidence. He told of how he and his wife had been quarrelling over the previous three weeks due to what he described as meddling and gossiping by folk who had no right to do so. He described how he and his wife had quarrelled again on Monday, 23 May and of how more meddling by a woman at the mill had caused them to row yet again as they headed home for their dinner break. He then told of how he had left home in order to return to the mill, expecting his wife to follow him shortly afterwards. Mr Kay, as one can imagine, was very upset by the gossip which had caused so many problems and he sadly told of how his wife failed to return to work that afternoon.

Mrs Davenport, a neighbour, also gave evidence and it was she who could shed some light on the events of that afternoon, when Sarah Kay should have been back at work. She noticed Mrs Kay approaching a field where young Mary Alice, her daughter, was playing with Mrs Davenport's little girl. It seems Mrs Davenport was taking care of Mary Alice while her parents were at work, so maybe there was a school holiday at the time, or maybe school had finished by then (the old newspaper accounts from the time failed to shed any light on this).

Mrs Davenport stated that Sarah Kay was not only in an agitated state, but that she was also in a hurry. She collected her child from the field and headed off with her in the direction of home. Mrs Davenport finished her testimony at this point and now it was the turn of Mrs Butterworth to testify on the tragic events of that afternoon.

On reaching home, Sarah Kay told her daughter to go next door to Mrs Butterworth's and ask to borrow a razor. Mrs Butterworth was visibly shaken as she told of these events, especially of how she had lent the razor to little Mary Alice, not suspecting anything sinister was about to occur. Mrs Butterworth watched as Mary Alice returned to her parents' cottage and in she went, with the door being locked behind her.

At this point it was Samuel Kay who took up the story. He told of how his wife had failed to return to work that afternoon and of how, at 6 p.m., he had finished his shift and returned home to find the doors locked. He had left his key at home when he went back to work after his dinner, expecting his wife to fetch hers when returning for the afternoon shift.

He knocked loudly at the door and Mrs Butterworth heard those knocks and came out of her cottage to see what was going on. Mrs Butterworth said to him that Sarah was 'not back from the mill yet' so he explained that she hadn't been back at work all afternoon. Mrs Butterworth was then visibly horrified, as she realised what had happened. 'Oh dear,' she said, 'the child fetched a razor from me.' Samuel Kay went off to get a neighbour, Henry Hayes, who brought along his ladder. Hayes put it to the bedroom window and went up to have a look in. What he witnessed was traumatic and he had the terrible ordeal of having to tell Samuel Kay that both his wife and stepdaughter were dead.

Another neighbour, John Howard, managed to get into the house through a window that had either been left open, or was forced open, and he unlocked the door. A doctor had been fetched by this time and he went upstairs to examine the bodies. Mother and daughter lay facing each other, and the pools of blood from each had merged into one. Sarah Kay had taken her daughter into the smallest bedroom of the house and there they had knelt down facing each other. Mrs Kay had then slit her daughter's throat, before cutting her own with much violence. They had both fallen close to each other, the razor lying where it dropped,

in-between them. The doctor explained that they were fearful wounds which had been inflicted by Mrs Kay, 'in a-frenzy'.

Samuel Kay explained that his wife had become very jealous, but that she had no grounds to be so. He also said that his wife had thought about suicide in the past after having quarrelled with her brother. He said that she had gone to one of the many mill lodges to be found in the area, intent on drowning herself, but a man fishing on the bank had put her off. The newspaper account went on to state that Samuel Kay seemed unconcerned at the inquest, unlike the witnesses who were very upset when giving their testimony. The jury now retired to consider their verdict, but not for long.

The jury quickly returned a verdict on Mrs Sarah Kay of willful murder and the destruction of herself while suffering from temporary insanity. The jury also took the unusual step of condemning the behavior of those persons who had meddled and gossiped about Mr Kay and who had spread the scandalous report that had eventually led to this tragedy. The inquest at the Bay Horse Inn now concluded and dispersed in silence.

The Case of a Bury Housewife

On Wednesday, 3 December 1884 Mr and Mrs Mason and their three children enjoyed breakfasting together before Mr Mason, a cotton-waste bleacher at a Bury mill, headed off to begin his day's work. All appeared normal at home and he got on with his work that morning, oblivious to the terrible goings-on at his home, which would soon change his life forever.

Hannah Mason was just 37 years of age when she committed suicide on the Wednesday morning, only 2 or 3 hours after her husband had left for work. Worse still, before killing herself she had also murdered her three children, standing by each of them and watching them fade away until they died. It was a tragedy that shocked all in the township with much more far-reaching effects felt after the national papers got hold of the story and reported it countrywide.

Two days later, on Friday, 5 December 1884, an inquest into the terrible event was held at the Church Inn, Elton, before the district coroner, Mr J.B. Edge. John Mason was called first in order to give evidence and he

A street at Elton today.

told those in attendance that he and Hannah Mason had been married for a number of years and that they lived on Milton Street, Elton, Bury. He had last seen his wife alive when he left for work at 8.30 a.m. on Wednesday 3 December. That was also the last time he had seen his three children alive. The eldest was Thomas Mason, who was 4 years of age; Nellie Mason was 3 years of age and the youngest child, Beatrice Mary, was only 18 months of age. Having been asked if his wife had been suicidal, he stated that she had not, nor had she made any threats regarding harming herself or her children. He did state, however, that she had been down for the past couple of weeks due to ill-health and that she had said to him that she could not see how she would ever get better. He then went on to tell his harrowing tale of how he discovered the bodies of his wife and three children later that day.

John Mason returned home every lunchtime in order to enjoy it with his wife. That day he arrived at his home in Milton Street at 12.30 p.m. as usual, but unusually the house was locked up and the blinds were down. Mr Mason hadn't taken a key to work with him, so he went to fetch his brother-in-law who lived at Bolton, but must have been in the Bury area, perhaps working, at the time. They forced open the back door of the property and lying on the table was a letter in Hannah Mason's handwriting, but they did not read it just then. Instead, they went upstairs and discovered the bodies of Mrs Mason and all three of the Mason children. A razor belonging to John Mason was lying on the floor next to the body of Mrs Mason. It was a gruesome and devastating discovery and John Mason struggled to hold himself together as he addressed the hearing and discussed the events in detail. He then told of how Dr Mellor and the police were sent for.

James Preston, Mason's brother-in-law, was the last witness to be called and he too described the events of that awful day, telling of how the bodies lay side by side, with all of their throats cut. Preston picked up the letter that was lying on the table and he said that this had blood on it, which indicated, along with the contents, that Mrs Mason had murdered her children before writing it. She had written:

> Dear John, You must forgive me for doing this. I have been a good wife to you. You must bury us all with George. I cannot leave my children behind to be knocked about. I say good-bye to all. I have done nothing wrong to anyone, and the Lord will forgive me. I have been a true wife to you. The cause of my illness I do not know. You have been a good husband to me. You must forgive me and try to forget. I have prayed to the Lord to take us. I could not lie in a sick-bed and die, and leave my children. I know the end of them. I watched them die and I am happy. Good-bye dear John. I have died happy and I know I have taken them all with me. Don't invite many to the funeral.

Dr Thomas Mellor of Elton gave evidence during the inquest, and he stated that all were quite dead when he arrived at the scene and examined the bodies. His opinion was that the children had been dead for approximately 2 hours, while the mother had been dead for approximately 1 hour. He then told of how he had seen her on Monday, only two days before these tragic events occurred. She had called at his surgery to tell him that she had been feeling ill for some time. He said she had been suffering with

Bolton Road, not far from the terrible murder and suicide at Elton.

dyspepsia, but that she was not seriously ill. She also told him that she had been studying about cancer of late and he noticed she had become obsessed with the illness and was convincing herself that she was suffering from cancer in some form and that she was going to die. He advised her to go out more in order to raise her spirits. He was of the opinion that she was not of a sound mind when she committed these terrible acts and that her brooding on cancer could have contributed to this.

Twelve-year-old Betsy Edmundson of Reaver Street, Bury, also appeared at the hearing. She told the packed room at the Church Inn that she had minded Mrs Mason's children that very morning between 9 and 10 a.m., and that she had not noticed anything was wrong with Mrs Mason. The jury went out to deliberate and quickly returned a verdict, concluding that Mrs Mason had murdered her children and then committed suicide while in a state of temporary insanity. The town of Bury continued to grieve after these shocking and terrible events had been heard and concluded at that spine-chilling inquest.

Additional Notes:

What struck me and left me a little baffled about this case, which was heard at that Elton inquest, was that Mrs Mason had included in her suicide letter the line that read: 'I cannot leave my children behind to be knocked about.' What did she mean by this? And, more importantly, why was this line not picked up on by those attending the inquest? This baffling line was not even discussed during the hearing, though no doubt many puzzled over it for weeks, and possibly months, afterwards. Did she mean that she could not possibly leave her children behind to be knocked about by life in general? Did she mean that she couldn't leave them behind because they may have been taken into the workhouse, or some other Victorian establishment infamous for the hardships and sufferings they brought on folk? Or, more to the point, did she mean that she couldn't leave them behind to be knocked about by their father, John Mason? Hannah Mason did state in her letter that her husband had been good to her, so this seems unlikely as men who knock children about usually knock their wives about too, though one cannot rule out this possibility. But why did no one question what she meant by that line?

The fact that no one questioned John Mason about his relationship with his children was undoubtedly due to the attitudes of those times. This was the Victorian era when children were often exploited in order to make life a little easier for adults. Children often worked in horrendous conditions in those days in order to bring in a few extra pence for the family, though poverty often made this a necessity. Parents needing extra money for ale and gambling were sometimes the motivating factors for sending children out to work and domestic problems such as violence towards wives and children was kept under wraps and not taken seriously by the authorities, with men being deemed far more important figures in society. Such prevailing attitudes no doubt contributed to the reason that John Mason was not questioned and cross-examined about that mysterious and provocative line in his wife's suicide letter.

The Case of a Bury Butcher

A married Bury butcher named Chadwick had been separated from his wife for a number of years and had been living with a lady named Stott for quite a long time, while his wife resided in a neighbouring town. Miss Stott left

Chadwick in early March of 1891 and on the 12th of that same month, about a week after they had separated, he pestered her yet again to be reconciled with him. She refused, telling him that their relationship was over. On the night of 12 March 1891, he followed Miss Stott to a house belonging to a Mrs Manock with whom she had been residing since leaving Chadwick, and there renewed his entreaties for her to come home, but again she flatly refused.

Exactly what had occurred to make her leave him and be so determined for them not to get back together was not reported, but her reasons may have been due to him being violent towards her. She could not have envisioned what would happen next, when she finally got through to him that any future reconciliation was absolutely out of the question.

Frustrated and in a rage, Chadwick went to a neighbouring butcher's shop and procured an incredibly sharp knife that was used for skinning carcasses. Again, reports at the time are rather scanty of details and it wasn't stated exactly how he managed to lay his hands on such a knife, but it seems he may well have known the butcher who owned this shop and had borrowed the knife from him, no doubt telling him that he needed it in order to carry out work at his own shop. Chadwick then returned to the home of Mrs Manock and somehow managed to get into a room alone with Miss Stott.

To her horror, her enraged former partner came at her with a knife and got her on the floor, where he pinned her down. He then used the knife to cut her from the side of her mouth right round to the base of her ear and both sides of her face, before stabbing her right through the heart. He then swiped the blade of the knife across his own throat, but failed to cause a lethal wound. He again attacked the dying Miss Stott, before taking a table knife and swiping it across his own throat yet again. This time the wound was lethal, as the knife cut so deep that it almost severed his head from his body. One can imagine the horrific scene that greeted Mrs Manock on her return home, and later the police when they were called to the tragic scene; two dead bodies and blood everywhere.

Chadwick had lived with Miss Stott for seven years and the town, and the whole of the country in fact, were shocked and horrified at the outcome of their relationship. An inquiry held soon after came to the conclusion that Chadwick had murdered Miss Stott and had committed suicide while suffering from temporary insanity.

The Case of a Bury Herbalist

Charles Alfred Hall was a much-respected medical herbalist who owned a thriving business in Bury which had been started by his grandfather and and that he had subsequently inherited from his father. On the morning of Tuesday, 20 October 1903, he went upstairs to the living room in order to light the fire, taking his son, Samuel Bernard Hall, with him. His wife, Susan Knight Hall, stayed downstairs to do the washing in the wash house behind the shop. It was about 11 a.m. when he and his son went upstairs, although his 5-year-old son quickly came back down in order to ask his mother for some matches. She gave the boy the box of matches and he returned upstairs to his father. Nothing more was heard until a customer came into the shop and was left unattended, which was unusual, as Mr Hall was a diligent shopkeeper and considered an expert in his field. He was usually always on hand to deal with any customers who came to his shop.

Mrs Hall apologised to the patiently waiting customer and called upstairs to her husband, whom she expected was probably having a little difficulty in getting the fire lit. There was no reply, nor any sound of movement. She made her way upstairs and found the living room vacant, so she went to look in the bedroom and was greeted by a horrific scene. Both her husband and son lay on separate beds and both were dead, with their throats cut and pools of blood soaking into the bed linen. The child was lying on a small bed with his throat cut so deeply it had also severed his windpipe and the father lay on a larger bed with the knife lying close to him. A note had been left on a nearby music cabinet. The reports of the time gave no indication of Mrs Hall's reaction on discovering this tragedy, but one can imagine how shocked and upset she was, possibly even hysterically so. She found the bodies at 11.30 a.m., exactly half an hour after her husband and son had gone upstairs to light the fire. The police and Dr Nuttall were called to the tragic scene and an inquest was held at Bury Police Court the very next day, on Wednesday, 21 October 1903.

Mrs Hall gave evidence at the inquest, which was remarkable when one considers the tragic events of the previous day, stating that her husband had been suffering with poor health for some time but would not consult a doctor. He had become quite deaf over recent months too and suspected that he had a bad heart, as he had suffered from frequent pains in his chest and head during recent weeks. Having been asked by the district coroner if her husband had been threatening suicide, or if his behavior had changed drastically of late, she replied that he had never mentioned taking his own life, nor had his behavior been any different. He seemed normal on that fateful morning and gave no clues as to how he was really feeling. He had been a little down because of his bad health, but seemed to be coping well enough with the difficulties he was experiencing. The contents of the note that had been left on the music cabinet were then read aloud to those in attendance, and Mrs Hall afterwards stated that she could not understand what her husband had written. The note read as follows: 'I know I have made a mistake in not taking him, but I trust to my Master above to right all. God help my poor wife. I hope she will forgive me as I would forgive even unto death. Susan, thou knows my wishes. C. Hall.'

Mill lodges at Tottington where Charles Alfred Hall often fished.

Dr Nuttall also gave evidence and explained how he had found a small cup at the scene which contained carbolic acid. The doctor believed that Mr Hall had drunk the acid immediately before killing himself. The general opinion of those who appeared to give their testimony at the inquest was that Mr Hall had a good reputation, was temperate in his habits and was quiet and honest. He ran a very respectable business and was also known as a keen fisherman, often seen angling on one of the reservoirs around Tottington village.

The jury did not take long to reach a decision and the verdict was read out after they had returned to the courtroom. It was decided that Charles Alfred Hall had murdered his child while suffering with an unsound mind and had then killed himself. There was silence for a few moments in the packed courtroom as all in attendance tried to come to terms with such terrible events; none more so than Mrs Hall, who was forced to grieve for both her husband and her innocent child.

Also from The History Press

BLOODY BRITISH HISTORY

Britain has centuries of incredible history to draw on – everything from Boudica and the Black Death to the Blitz. This local series, harking back to the extraordinary pulp magazines of days gone by, contains only the darkest and most dreadful events in your area's history. So embrace the nastier side of British history with these tales of riots and executions, battles and sieges, murders and regicides, witches and ghosts, death, devilry and destruction!

Also from The History Press

GRIM ALMANAC

The *Grim Almanac* series is a day-by-day catalogue of ghastly tales from history. Full of dreadful deeds, macabre deaths and bizarre tragedies, each almanac includes captivatingly diverse tales of highwaymen, smugglers, murderers, bodysnatchers, duellists, poachers, witches, rioters and rebels, as well as accounts of old lock-ups, prisons, bridewells and punishments. All these, plus tales of accidents by land, sea and air, and much more, are here. If you have ever wondered about the nasty goings-on of yesteryear, then look no further – it's all here. But do you have the stomach for it?

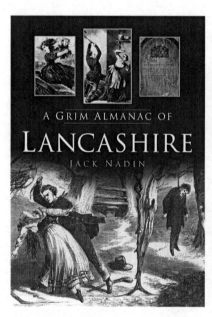

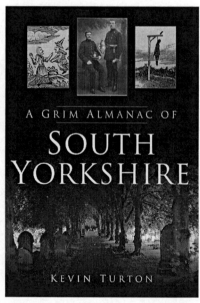

Also from The History Press

We are proud to present our history crime fiction imprint, The Mystery Press, featuring a dynamic and growing list of titles written by diverse and respected authors, united by the distinctiveness and excellence of their writing. From a collection of thrilling tales by the CWA Short Story Dagger award-winning Murder Squad, to a Victorian lady detective determined to solve some sinister cases of murder in London, these books will appeal to serious crime fiction enthusiasts as well as those who simply fancy a rousing read.

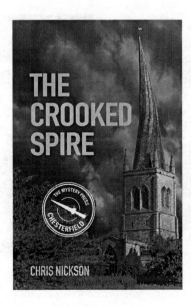

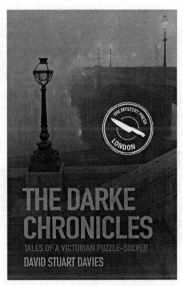

Find these titles and more at
www.thehistorypress.co.uk

Also from The History Press

GREATER MANCHESTER

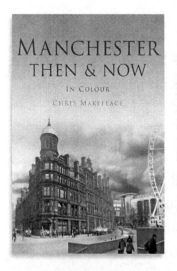

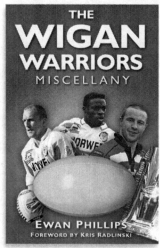

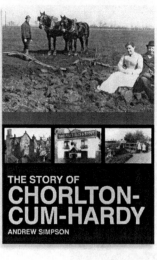

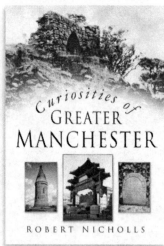

Also from The History Press

WHEN DISASTER STRIKES

9 780752 488714